Countdown To Retirement For Educators

0-944223-00-1

Countdown To Retirement For Educators

By Wilson Riles
and Jessie Heinzman

BoothMark Books
MOONLIGHT PRESS
Westminster California

This publication is designed to provide accurate and authoritative information in regard to the subject matter covered. It is sold with the understanding that the publisher is not engaged in rendering legal, accounting or other professional service. If legal advice or other expert assistance is required, the services of a competent professional person should be sought.

Printed in the United States of America.

First printing, 1988.   1 2 3 4 5 6 7 8 9

Library of Congress Cataloging-In-Publication Data
Riles, Wilson C.
        Countdown to retirement for educators /
by Wilson Riles and Jessie Heinzman
              p.   cm.

        Bibliography: p.
        Includes Index.
        ISBN 0-944223-00-1 (pbk.) : $9.95
        1. Teachers —United States—Retirement.
2. Teachers—United States—Finance, Personal
I. Heinzman, Jessie, 1915-
II. Title.
LB2844.1.R5R54   1988   371.1'0068'3—dc19   87-12450
                                                        CIP

BoothMark Books
Moonlight Press
Box 994
Westminster CA 92684-0994

Contents

Continuing Education. Travel And Learn.
Learn At Home. Cultural Events. Summary.

11. Retire To Community Service   141
Volunteers. Federally Sponsored Volunteer
Programs. Museums Need You. Social Service.
Jury Duty. Teacher's Aide. Tutor. Boards And
Commissions. Organizations. League Of
Women Voters. Political Parties And Pressure
Groups. Churches. Summary.

12. Share Your Knowledge For Pay   155
Consulting. Writing. Multi-Level Marketing.
Real Estate. Summary.

13. Have Fun   164
Sports. Hobbies. Travel. Preparation.
Imagination. Money Saving Tips. When To Go.

About The Authors

Wilson Riles is uniquely qualified to explore the concerns of retirement for professional educators. For 12 years, he served as superintendent of public instruction for the state of California. The leadership he provided to the public school system came during three terms of unprecedented challenges to the state's and the nation's educational resources and programs.

National recognition earned during his service as state superintendent led to his role as president of the Council of Chief State School Officers and as advisor to four presidents on national educational issues. He has worked closely with the business community, serving as a trustee for the Foundation for Teaching Economics and as a director of Wells Fargo Bank and Pacific Gas and Electric Company.

Earning his bachelor and master degrees from Northern Arizona University, Dr. Riles also is holder of honorary doctorates from nine prestigious colleges and universities from throughout the United States. His early days in the classroom were during the 1940s and early '50s as an elementary school teacher and administrator in Arizona.

He retired to an active life from the California statehouse in 1982, becoming president of his own Wilson Riles and Associates, Inc., an educational consultant firm with headquarters in Sacramento, California.

Wilson Riles has been a consultant for United Resources, an Integrated Resources company which provides financial services and products to the education profession. This book was developed in connection with his work for United Resources and parts of it have been excerpted in many of the company's periodicals and publications.

Jessie Heinzman, who earned her bachelor and master degrees from California State University in Sacramento, retired to an active multi-faceted career after 30 years of state service and five years with Sacramento county.

Since departing regular employment in 1975, she has assisted in forming a local unified school district and served as interim superintendent, has taught as a volunteer in a local private high school, and accepted appointment to the Mendocino County board of education.

During the 12-year period since her retirement, she has earned the background to be a travel consultant in the field of low-cost holidays, developed during numerous self-catering holidays she has undertaken in Europe and the South Pacific.

When Jessie Heinzman writes about the advantages of preparation for retirement, she knows the truth of what she says from actual experience. She began her preparation to enjoy being "gainfully unemployed" in 1938, the year she started work for the state of California and learned about the state's retirement policies.

I.
Introduction

1 Popular Misconceptions About Retirement

Many younger educators are willing to spend time planning next summer's vacation. Yet, they are unwilling to spend time planning for retirement. Why do they have such reluctance to follow the advice they constantly give to their students: Prepare today for the opportunities of tomorrow? The answer is not hard to find.

In case you haven't noticed, retirement is getting a bad rap. The media, hooked on youth, doesn't seem able to resist perpetuating myths about the horrors of life after work.

It's time to blow the whistle on the doomsayers. It's time to expose the myths and misconceptions about retirement and to alleviate the fear that weakens the will to face the future. It's time to start tomorrow's gainfully unemployed on their plans for *Freedom*.

To begin our planning, we need to take stock of where we are. What do you really know about retirement?

1

	True	False
People die soon after they retire	____	____
Retired people have no value to society	____	____
Retired people live below the poverty line	____	____
Retired people are bored and boring	____	____
Retirement and senility are synonymous	____	____

Now for the facts.

People Die Soon After They Retire

The life expectancy of the average 60-year old is 18.8 years for females and 14.4 years for males. Educators are better educated than the average. They have more knowledge about nutrition and health, and have had the time and health insurance coverage to take care of health problems early. These advantages give educators a much greater life expectancy than the average.

At 60, a female educator can expect to live 27.8 years, a male educator can expect to live 24.4 years. In a decade from now those life expectancies will increase by about one year; in two decades, the increase will be about two years. That means that a 40-year old educator planning to retire at 60 can look forward to nearly 30 years of life after retirement. That is a far cry from death soon after retirement.

In California, the State Teachers Retirement System reports that the average age of present retired teachers is 88. Many of California's retired educators are over the century mark. If you are going to have that many years post retirement, you need to prepare for them during your working life.

Retired People Have No Value To Society

Books, magazines, the Sunday supplements and television specials delight in portraying the miserable plight of senior citizens. The media fill newspapers and television screens with the collective misery of bag ladies, derelicts, and abused nursing home residents. Old people are alienated from mainstream society. Their children have no time for them. Their grandchildren rarely visit. Friends are dead. Shop clerks push old people aside and wait upon them last. No one wants to hear what the old have learned through experience. If there is one thing old is, it's useless.

That picture of the retired may sell books and attract viewers who sympathize momentarily. For the average over-60 population it is seldom true. For retired educators that picture is pure fiction.

Retired educators must work to avoid the hundreds of opportunities waiting to occupy their every waking moment. Because the normal source of volunteers for charitable and cultural organizations has disappeared with the rush of women into the labor market, these groups court the retiree with a devotion that would delight any person seeking employment. If you think the retired educational professionals are sitting at home watching paint dry, check museums, classrooms, and day care centers. You will find them there. Check the "board watchers," the jury boxes, the school boards, the PTA, the hospitals and the little theater groups. You will find them there.

Check the Foster Grandparent program, the Peace Corps, the League of Women Voters, the Lions and Rotary clubs, the fraternal organizations. Again, you will find them there. Society does value retired people, particularly retired educational professionals.

Jane B., who spent 40 years teaching third grade, is a docent at the local art museum. She delights in explaining the works of the masters to youngsters on field trips. She makes every child aware of the beauty captured in oil, watercolor, and sculpture. Jane does more than awaken children to the joy of art. She is learning through museum classes to appreciate the subtle nuances of art works she used to simply view with pleasure. She is growing mentally every year in a field new to her. She has become one the museum's most valued staff members.

John G., who moved from the classroom to administration many years before he retired, decided to try the other side of school governance. He ran for and was elected to the school district governing board where he serves with distinction, admired by both the taxpayers and school personnel.

Belle H., dean of women at the local community college for more years than she cared to remember, decided at age 70 that women belonged in politics. After retirement she ran for mayor of her city and was elected with a resounding majority. She served three terms of four years each before she moved on to less strenuous retirement as a volunteer counselor to young college women seeking careers in public service.

Fred M., a retired high school math teacher, is now running a successful computer consulting firm. He has combined his knowledge of mathematics with his love for personal computers to become a problem solver for many small businesses struggling to adapt to the demands of high technology. Fred spends his free time on the cutting edge of his field. He is in demand all over his state as a seminar leader because he not only knows the things computers are capable of doing and handling today, but also what they will be able to do tomorrow.

Mary S., a social studies teacher, traveled widely after she retired. By the time she reached 75, her reduced resources required that she quit roaming the world. It took Mary only weeks after her last around-the-world trip to find the Foster Grandparents program. She has worked for the past ten years with troubled youth in the local juvenile hall. Her family wishes she could go back to traveling. Nevertheless, Mary and her kids, as she calls them, are enjoying a rewarding relationship.

None of these examples is unique. Active, retired educators all over America are contributing, as they always have, to the well being of society. They have value to society and they have all the ego satisfaction they formerly enjoyed through gainful employment.

Retired People Live Below The Poverty Line

In 1987 the poverty rate for persons 65-plus was 12.4 percent. That was less than the rate for persons under 65 (14.7 percent). Another 8 percent of the elderly were classified as "near poor." This means that 79 percent of the 65-plus were comfortably above the poverty level. The official poverty level is $7,400 for an older couple and $5,500 for an older person living alone. The majority of retired educators now live above the poverty line. This is not to say that an educator who retires today, relying solely on a teacher's retirement system annuity, might not fall below an official poverty line sometime in the future. Too many educators who retired in the 1950s or early 1960s believed that they would live out their lives comfortably with incomes between $5,000 and $10,000. Those incomes which placed them in the "well off" category at retirement are now drastically eroded by inflation. In another decade those incomes may well place them below the poverty line. Even with modest inflation a fixed income can lose 50 percent of its purchasing power in 10 years. A severe cycle of inflation obviously could reduce the purchas-

5

ing power of that income by even greater amounts.

A retirement handbook published in 1960 reported that retirees could buy small comfortable retirement homes throughout the United States for prices ranging from $8,500 to $15,000. The same book suggested that a monthly retirement income of $500 would be adequate for a couple. Forty-year old educators in 1960, planning retirement in 1988 based on these figures, would find themselves in desperate circumstances today. That modest retirement home now costs 10 times as much as it did in 1960.

Retired educators do not need to anticipate that retirement means poverty. Nevertheless, in view of the estimated length of life after retirement and the uncertainty of future inflationary trends, they must exercise care to avoid the possibility.

Retired People Are Bored And Boring

Carl Megel, past president of the American Federation of Teachers, wrote in the introduction to his book, *Planning For Retirement*: "The success of your retirement years depends largely upon your outlook before you approach retirement. Your career in education has taught you planning, discipline, and ingenuity—skills that can easily be applied to make your retirement years happy and productive." Megel, at 85, is far from bored or boring. He still puts in a fair day's work at AFT Washington headquarters. He campaigns vigorously for candidates known to be sympathetic to the cause of education and he lobbies constantly for better schools.

In its recruitment brochure "Older Americans of the Peace Corps," the U.S. Peace Corps' Office of Marketing illustrates the value of teachers in the program: "Virginia Spray, 71, of Burden, Kansas, helped Liberian children receive a better education. Virginia, who completed her master's degree in education at age 60, had taught school for 27 years before becoming a Peace Corps volunteer. 'I was getting in a rut,' she said. Her volunteer assignment was to conduct teacher-training workshops. She began by visiting local schools in a town not too far from Monrovia, the capital of Liberia. 'What I found in one school was 60 children sitting on logs in one room. There were no textbooks,' she added. She began to collect old books from the U.S. school where she had taught and gave them to the students.... Virginia shared a mudblock house with another volunteer. They cooked on a one burner, kerosene stove and got their water from a hydrant. People called her 'Old Ma,' a term of endearment. 'I had a wonderful experience. Age is so looked up to, you suddenly feel important again'."

Virginia is not bored nor is she boring. She is typical of the many retired teachers who have volunteered to serve in either the Peace Corps or in VISTA, the domestic service branch of ACTION.

Those who are not so daring are finding life equally exciting in their home communities. A hobby of handweaving led retired educator Bob S. and his wife into a senior cooperative craft program. They share in the operation of a store in the historic area of their city where they and other seniors offer their handicrafts for sale. They not only have an opportunity to earn extra income from their weaving but meet and talk with visitors from all over the world. "It's even more educational than teaching," Bob says.

He and his wife can dine out for months on their tales of people they have met in the shop and the problems foreigners have with our language and customs. Bob S. doesn't look or feel 90. He and his wife are planning a trip soon to Africa to visit a family they met in the shop and entertained in their home. Neither bored nor boring, the couple is constantly looking for opportunities to learn new languages and to try new experiences.

Retirement And Senility Are Synonymous

A small number (1.3 million) and percentage (5 percent) of the total 65-plus population lived in institutions (primarily nursing homes) in 1980. That 5 percent represents an average. When broken down by age group the percentage ranged from 2 percent for persons 65-74 years to 7 percent for persons 75-84 years. The percentage went up to 23 for persons 85-plus. Stated another way, over 90 percent of the population between 65 and 84 were living outside of institutions in 1980. More than three-quarters of those over 80 were able to live independent lives.

These data, from AARP's *Profile of Older Americans: 1984,* are a strong rebuttal to the popular myth that retired people are unable to care for themselves.

Quite frequently symptoms of senility are simply confusion brought on by medication or lack of stimulating experiences. Senility is not the inevitable consequence of either aging or retirement if you maintain good health and remain mentally active.

Moving From Myths To Reality

To summarize: People die soon after retirement...False. Retired people have no value to society...False. Retired people live below the poverty line...False. Retired people are bored and boring...-False. Retirement and senility are synonymous-...False. Retirement should really be called commencement...True.

Will you be ready for *Freedom?* Whatever you desire, planning can make the difference between a retirement that fulfills your dreams and one of disappointment and frustration.

2 Importance Of Prior Planning

I f you had a fairy godmother who could grant you the three things you most want for yourself after retirement, you probably would ask for wealth, health and time to enjoy them.

You do have a fairy godmother—you. It is within your power to make your three wishes come true. All you have to do is decide on your goals and plan what you must do to achieve them. Then, year by year, as you countdown to retirement, put those plans into operation.

"It's not that easy," you say. "I have bills to pay now. I have children to raise and send to college. My parents will need help as they grow old. I have all I can do now to keep my head above water. Why should I worry now about something that won't happen for years?"

Retirement may seem far off but it is as certain as death and taxes. Some of us may marry, some may divorce. Some of us may spend our entire working life

9

in the classroom, others may become administrators. Some of us may greet every working day with enthusiasm, others may burn out and simply mark time. Whether we want to face the fact or put it out of mind, we are all going to retire one day. The question is simply what to do to prepare for the inevitable.

Decide at 30 what kind of life you want for the 25 or 30 years you will live after 60 and you will have 360 months to prepare for that lifestyle. Decide at 57 and you will have only 36 months to accumulate the resources you will need to make your dreams come true.

Think of the years ahead, not as the time before retirement, but as a "Countdown to Freedom." Each year gives you an opportunity to accumulate the health, the capital and the activities you need to assure a carefree life after you leave the work force. Each decade gives you an opportunity to make mid-course corrections. Finally, you are at "D (departure) day," prepared to say with joy, "Free at last." Talk to retired educators and you will find that those who planned ahead are the ones who have achieved satisfaction and independence in their retirement years. Planning, they will tell you, helps you to control events rather than having events control you.

You Are In Charge
Your countdown to freedom starts with a time line:

Now (date)	_____
Retirement (date)	_____
Months to go	_____

Post that time line now on the refrigerator door. Count down those remaining months. It's later than you think.

Goals

You need first to ask yourself a few questions about what retirement means to you.

Have you decided that you want retirement to be a time of slowing down, a time spent with family and friends in a familiar location?

Have you decided that you want retirement to be a chance for a new career? Will retirement be an opportunity to do what you have always wanted to do but never had the time?

Have you decided that you want retirement to mean that you will finally have a chance to travel?

Before you commit yourself to a goal, be certain that it is congruent with your personality.

Ask yourself:

Do I hesitate to try new things?
Do I fear or dislike the unknown?
Do I enjoy different peoples and cultures?
Do I become homesick easily?
Am I a joiner or a loner?
Am I shy or outgoing?
Am I a risk taker or cautious?
Am I a life-long learner?

The goal of travel is not for you if you don't want to be uprooted from familiar surroundings. If the contrary is true, you may well want to join the ranks of those retirees who delight in wanderlust.

Are you flexible? Are you comfortable with uncertainty? Then your chances of having a successful new career after retirement are great enough to make that your goal.

These questions are not the only ones you should ask yourself. They suggest only the direction your thinking should take before you set your goals. Keep in mind as you make early decisions that time and circumstances may change your mind. By starting the planning process early enough, you have time for interim corrections.

Now to get back to those three primary goals for retirement: health, wealth and time to enjoy them.

Health

What is the state of your health now? Do you have good health habits? Here is a short quiz to measure your awareness of measures which lead to good health:

	True	False
I have a family doctor whom I see regularly	___	___
I do not neglect health problems	___	___
I do not smoke	___	___
I do not use drugs	___	___
I limit my use of alcohol	___	___
I exercise regularly	___	___
I maintain good posture	___	___
I eat a balanced diet	___	___
I am at or near my recommended weight	___	___
I am protecting my bones from osteoporosis	___	___
I avoid foods high in cholesterol	___	___
I practice good oral hygiene	___	___
I see my dentist regularly	___	___
I do not expose my hearing to loud sounds	___	___
I have my vision checked regularly	___	___

If you respond to these questions in the affirmative, you have a good chance of reaching retirement sound of wind and limb. If you respond in the negative, you may fall victim to one of the health hazards of the older American: heart disease, cardiovascular disease, cancer, arthritis, osteoporosis, back problems, loss of vision, hearing or teeth. Almost all of these health problems can be forestalled or ameliorated by early detection and/or good health habits.

During your countdown to retirement your plans should include measures to keep physically fit. Loss of sight, hearing and mobility are three of the four most threatening physical problems of the aging process. The fourth, and frequently the most worrisome problem, is loss of mental capacity.

Dr. Berwic Wright writing in *Choice*, quotes Rudyard Kipling,

"The camel's hump is an ugly hump,
As well you may see at the zoo.
Uglier yet is the hump we may get
From having too little to do."

Wright continues his article by saying: "People need people. They need to be wanted and to be able to contribute. One of the necessities of retirement planning, particularly for someone coming from full time employment, is the need to replace the personal associations and identity provided by work.... Retirement is change and change is threatening.... A competent person who has too little to do becomes frustrated and stressed. In these terms boredom can be regarded as underemployment and we know medically that such people tend to become depressed and irritable, perhaps drink too much and become ill from any disease that is going around."

Those who postpone thinking about and planning for post retirement activity until "D day" has arrived find

Dr. Wright is right. Certainly you will find your retirement years happier if you are in good health to start with. Chapter 7 will assist you with post-retirement health maintenance.

Health without wealth has its drawbacks, too.

Wealth

There are some basic sources for building a foundation for financial independence.

	Yes	No
Are you covered by a state teacher's retirement plan?	____	____
Are you covered by social security?	____	____
Does your union offer retirement benefits?	____	____
Do you have a payroll deduction plan for credit union or other savings?	____	____
Do you put money into tax sheltered annuities?	____	____
Are you buying your own home?	____	____

Affirmative answers to these questions mean that you have taken the first steps toward making your second goal a reality.

Will you be rich when you retire?

Certainly no one goes into teaching to become wealthy, unless he or she is the victim of some very bad counseling. By the time you retire you will have contributed generously to others; then it will be time for you to be good to yourself. Nevertheless, it will take a great deal of planning and persistence to assure yourself of financial independence. You will have to make many decisions between now and retirement to keep a financial plan up-to-date. Chapters 3, 4 and 5 will help you plan your financial strategy.

You now have some idea of what needs to be done to bring you to your goals of health and wealth. You need to give some thought to the prior planning required to make the best use of the time you will have in those years of freedom.

Time On Your Hands

Carl Megel in his foreword to *Planning For Retirement* tells of his experiences in encouraging educators to pre-plan their retirements:

"I remember specifically talking to a teacher who was telling me how much he was looking forward to retirement within the next few years. When I asked him where he planned to live, he said he would probably go to Florida. Further discussion revealed that this individual had never been to Florida, had neither friends nor relatives in Florida, and knew nothing about the climate, the prices or value of property there.

"Other teachers talked about their plans for traveling after retirement. Again, I found that most of them knew very little about where they wished to go, neither possessing knowledge of travel costs nor how they would move about once they arrived at their destination. Many failed to realize that the travel they anticipated demands good physical condition, which at age 35 offers few problems, but at retirement age might be too demanding."

Jack S. and his wife are typical of those Carl Megel writes about. They too thought Florida was the ideal retirement location. They sold their home in the middle west when they retired. They left friends, family, and familiar surroundings and moved into a mobile home in a retirement community in Florida. They soon found they hated the climate, were tired of inactivity and were almost friendless. They missed the intellectual stimulus of the college town where they had lived most of their lives. Their decision to move back to their old community was costly. They lost money on the sale of their mobile home. They had to spend much of their savings to make a down payment on a home in their former community. Worst of all they were unprepared for the large house payments they had to make. They might have avoided the trauma caused by a year of upheaval and disappointment, if they had planned ahead, tried living in Florida during school holidays and had rented their home instead of selling it.

A travel agent warned another couple considering retirement to the Caribbean, "Don't. You will drink your daily bottle of cheap rum around sun-down by the end of the first year. By the third year, you will have finished it before noon."

On the other hand, Bill and Mary J. planned for years for their retirement to another area. They dedicated each winter vacation to exploring possible places to live. When they found a likely place, they visited it again during the summer vacation to see if they would enjoy the place all year round. They narrowed the possibilities down to three by the time they retired. They then leased their home, rented quarters in one of the places under consideration and stayed for a year. They spent the next year in the second of the initial choices, the third year in the last. By the end of the third year, Bill and Mary knew where they wanted to live. They knew how much it would cost to live there and they acquired friends who would form a new network of support and had identified activities which they could enjoy as they grew older.

They kept their former home leased, using the income to supplement their retirement benefits. The tax benefits of owning and personally managing rental property helped to shelter other income. Bill and Mary needed no fairy godmother to grant them happiness. They had health, wealth and time to enjoy both. It was neither luck or magic. They planned it that way.

Studies show that the majority of retired people do not relocate. They stay in the communities where they have families and friends. They choose to keep their mortgage-free homes. Their homes were purchased before the ravages of inflation and high interest rates pushed housing costs to their present heights. Those who stay in familiar surroundings often find they are suddenly at loose ends. They have no reason to get up in the morning, no ego-building activity to give meaning to their day. They have left the cage but don't know how to fly.

Freedom from the obligation to report to work five days a week, freedom from fear of losing your job, freedom from financial worries can be either a golden opportunity or a burden.

It is important that you think about what you will do to occupy that 50 hours or so a week that you formerly spent working and commuting. It is imperative that you have a plan ready for implementation on "D day." A wise man once said, "Killing time is suicide on the installment plan." Unless you prepare for activity, one day fades into another and you waste your best years. As educators know better than anyone else: a human mind is a terrible thing to waste.

During the countdown to retirement it is just as important to plan how you are going to spend your post retirement years as it is to plan for health and wealth. Chapters 8 through 13 will give you some ideas about making the best possible use of your mind and your time.

Planning, whether it is for physical fitness, for financial security, for adventure, for a new career or for a change of lifestyle, can enable you to make choices.

That's what this book is all about: choices. You are a series of choices. You choose what to eat, think and do every day. Therefore you do have the choice to have the life of your choice. The remaining chapters will help you to use your countdown years to choose to your best advantage.

II
Countdown

3 *Financial Independence*

Your fears of the unknown will diminish once you put on paper realistic estimates of how much you will need to provide financial independence and how much income you will have to reach that goal. In this chapter you will concentrate on how much you will need. Remember that neither man nor woman can live by bread alone. You should cover not only the necessities of life in your planning, but also those items beyond the basics which make the difference between "retirement: a golden opportunity" and "retirement: a dismal burden."

How Much Do I Need

Most authorities agree that you will need at least 60 to 70 percent of your regular take-home pay to have a financially independent and comfortable retirement. The exact amount will vary. It will depend upon the age at which you retire, the place you choose to live after retirement, your state of health, and what you want to do with your freedom.

The amount is based on your take-home pay for three simple reasons. You no longer will make contributions to your pension fund and social security. Your income taxes may be reduced. You no longer will be paying into your tax sheltered annuity or other automatic savings plan.

You may want to supplement your retirement income by either a full- or part-time job if you retire early. If you desire to live in a high-cost urban area in the northeast your expenses will be higher than if you choose to live in a rural area in one of the sunbelt states. Your medical expenses will be higher if you are in poor health or do not have adequate health insurance or Medicare. These expenses will add to your total cost of living. If you prefer to travel widely after retirement, or to engage in an active social life in a resort community, for example, that lifestyle will be costly. Each of us must modify estimates of average costs by personal differences.

Ask yourself now:

What are my present monthly expenses?
What will I need each month after I retire?
What will inflation do to my plans?

If you don't know the answers to these questions (few of us do without some calculation) the following material will help you.

Basic Needs

The U.S. Department of Labor's Bureau of Labor Statistics (BLS) provides the following budget breakdown in percentages of gross income for the average retired couple.

Use these figures to make your own estimates.

Housing	33%
Food	29%
Clothing and personal care	7%
Transportation	10%
Medical care	10%
Other family consumption	5%
Other	6%
Total	100%

What do those categories listed by the BLS cover? Here is its explanation:

Category	Items to include
Housing	Rental fees, home or apartment ownership expenses such as mortgage payments, home insurance, real estate taxes, utility costs, home upkeep and repair costs, condominium fees.
Food	Grocery and liquor expenses, meals eaten away from home, cost of entertaining others in your home.
Clothing	Cost of new clothes, laundry and dry cleaning, alterations, shoe repair.
Transportation	Charges for gasoline, car upkeep, repair, car payments, insurance, license fees, bus and taxi fares, vacation driving, parking fees.

Medical care

Out-of-pocket payments for doctor, dentist, and hospital; medicine, prescription and non-prescription; health insurance payments.

Other family
   Consumption

Family recreation costs, household furnishings, appliances, pocket money, reading matter, stamps, etc.

Other

Religious and charitable donations, life insurance, gifts, savings, income taxes.

To illustrate what those BLS percentages mean in terms of dollars spent, consider two couples and one single parent: first, the Smiths,* a typical retired couple; second, the Wilsons,* retired educators, and third, Abbey,* also a retired educator. The Smiths have an income of $10,000, the Wilsons, $30,000 and Abbey $20,000.

The Wilsons and Abbey probably spend lower percentages of their income on food and shelter and higher percentages on such categories as "Transportation," "Other Family Consumption" and "Other." The rule is: the higher your income bracket, the lower the proportion you must spend on necessities and the more you will have left for extras such as travel and recreation.

Make an estimate of needs at retirement using 70 percent of your current take-home pay as if it were your retirement income. Apply the BLS percentages to find what you might be spending if you were retired.

---

*Names have been changed to protect privacy.

Comparison Budgets

Budget Category	Percent of income	Smiths	Wilson	Abbey
Housing	33%	$3,300	$9,900	$6,600
Food	29%	2,900	8,700	5,800
Clothing & Personal Care	7%	700	2,100	1,400
Transportation	10%	1,000	3,000	2,000
Medical Care	10%	1,000	3,000	2,000
Other Family Consumption	5%	500	1,500	1,000
Other	6%	600	1,800	1,200
Totals	100%	$10,000	$30,000	$20,000

Were your estimates close to those of the Wilsons or to Abbey's? No? The reason is simple. Your estimates reflect your personal circumstances and preferences. This is as it should be. No one is really average, not the Smiths, not the Wilsons, not Abbey, not you. Use average or typical cases only as reference points.

You need to do a little homework to refine your estimates of basic needs at retirement.

Housing

The Bureau of Labor Statistics includes many items within the broad category "housing." Use those items to analyze your present expenditures and to make an estimate of your needs after you retire. To help you to see what questions you need to ask, we will visit two hypothetical families, the Joneses, both educators with one child; and the Miller family, a single parent with two sons.

First, consider the Jones family. They are both 55. They plan to retire in 10 years. Their child is in the second year of the state university which is in their home town. The Joneses have been teaching for 20 years. They bought their home 20 years ago. They have a 25-year mortgage. They live in California. Assuming that they will receive only cost of living increases of 2 percent a year for the next 10 years, the Joneses can anticipate a retirement annuity of $43,883 when they retire in 1995.

What are the Joneses spending for shelter now? What will they need after retirement?

	Now	*After Retire- ment
Mortgage payments	$3,600	$ 0
Rental fees	0	0
Home insurance	500	1,036
Real estate taxes	500	610
Utility costs	950	1,850
Home upkeep and repair costs	500	740
Condominium fees	0	0
Totals	$ 6,050	$ 4,236

* Projected

The Joneses both teach in the same district. In the same place on the salary schedule, they each are receiving $30,000 each, gross pay. The percentage of their take-home pay going for shelter now is far less than the percentages paid by younger couples who bought after the spurt in real estate prices and interest rates.

The Joneses belong to the lucky generation. They can retire at 65 with a home worth several times what they paid for it. They can continue to live where they are and spend between 9 and 10 percent of their basic retirement income on shelter. Or they can sell their home when they are 65 and pay no capital gains tax on the first $125,000 profit. They can then buy a smaller house or condo in some other area, if they want to relocate.

Mary Miller, our single parent, has only her own income to support herself and her two boys. She divorced when the boys were young. She has never received child support payments on a regular basis. She was married long enough to qualify for spousal benefits from her former husband's social security account. Nevertheless, changes in the law will eliminate that as a source of retirement income since she is eligible for a state pension. She is 45 and has been teaching secondary school for 20 years. She plans to retire at 60. At that time her boys will be through school and on their own.

She sold her home when the boys started at the state university in another area. She is using the interest from her equity invested in a tax-exempt bond fund plus some of her current income to support them while they attend college. She has been living alone in a small apartment near the high school where she teaches.

	Now	*After retire-ment
Rental fees	$6,000	$8,644
Mortgage payments	0	0
Home insurance	0	0
Real estate taxes	0	0
Utility costs	300	540
Home upkeep and repair costs	0	0
Totals	$6,400	$9,364

* Projected

27

What is Miller spending for shelter now? What will she need after retirement?

Miller has a bachelor of arts degree plus 90 units and a master's degree. She is at the top of her district's salary schedule. She receives $40,000 gross pay. Miller can anticipate a retirement annuity of $37,684 when she leaves teaching in the year 2000. As with most teachers, her salary, once she has reached the top of the salary schedule, will fall behind actual increases in the cost of living. She is paying a larger percentage of her income for shelter than the Joneses, but far below the percentages paid by persons in lower income brackets. Miller, too, is one of the lucky generation, the generation which bought homes in the mid-60s and saw their ordinary $30,000 tract homes escalate in price to $100,000 by 1984.

The decision to sell and not to buy another property was costly from the standpoint of taxation. She had to pay capital gains tax on the profit from the sale of her home. On the other hand, she was able to protect the amount she had saved in her tax sheltered annuity.

Miller was fortunate to find an apartment for $500 a month. She would have to pay over $600 for a similar unit in a large urban area where the cost of living is higher. You will probably find that you too, are one of the lucky ones when you analyze your present and future needs for shelter.

You should consult the Inflation Impact chart in the Appendix to adjust your estimates from now to your retirement date. Use the factor listed opposite the number of years you have to go to retirement under the average inflation you think will prevail. For example, if you have 10 years to go before "D day" find 10 in the column to the left, follow the row across until it intersects with the average annual inflation you think will take place between now and then. Multiply your present figures by that factor. Before you panic, remember to adjust your present salary by your expected movement across and down your salary schedule to arrive at your final salary in terms of 1988 dollars. You can compute your anticipated retirement annuity by modifying that figure, as we did in the case of the Joneses and Miller. You will, of course, have to use the formula in effect in your state. Keep in mind some expenses will not go up quite as fast as the cost of living; others will increase more rapidly. Overall, however, total costs rise at the average inflation rate.

Food

The BLS includes several items under Food. Use the list below to analyze where you are now and where you will be when you retire. We will again use the Jones family to illustrate the changes you may expect.

	Now	*After retire- ment
Groceries	$8,320	$7,697
Liquor	200	297
Meals eaten away from home	3,000	740
Cost of entertaining others in your home	600	888
Totals	$12,120	$9,622

* Projected

The Joneses are in a high income bracket. They therefore spend less than the so-called normal percentage for their food. Their retirement needs for food will be about half of their present needs before adjusting for inflation. They will eat fewer meals away from home, thus substantially reducing that item. There will be two instead of three to feed when their child leaves home. They will purchase fewer convenience foods. Jane Jones will have time to prepare food instead of relying so heavily on packaged foodstuffs.

The Joneses are a family of three now, reducing to two in a few years. Miller is a family of one, as her sons are away at school. She will see some change in her food budget when she retires for the same reason as the Joneses: fewer meals eaten away from home, fewer convenience foods.

Here is her food budget before and after retirement:

	Now	*After retire-ment
Groceries	$2,600	$3,601
Liquor	25	45
Meals eaten away from home	1,000	900
Cost of entertaining others in your home	300	540
Totals	$3,925	$5,086

* Projected

Neither Miller nor the Joneses are coming close to the 29 percent of income that the BLS feels is typical. You probably won't either, but it is a calculation you need to make to discover your own percentage.

Clothing

Referring to the BLS explanation of the broad budget category Clothing we find a short list of items.

You will find the list helpful in your effort to learn how much you spend in this category. We will illustrate clothing expenses by looking at the Joneses' and Miller's outlays now and after retirement.

Jones	Now	*After retire- ment
New clothes	$2,760	$1,036
Laundry	0	0
Dry cleaning	350	148
Alterations	30	0
Shoe repair	50	37
Totals	$3,190	$1,221

Miller	Now	*After retire- ment
New clothes	$ 800	$ 540
Laundry	156	279
Dry cleaning	175	135
Alterations	0	0
Shoe repair	30	27
Totals	$1,161	$ 981

* Projected

Taxes

One of the significant items in your present budget which will change when you retire is the amount you will pay for federal and state income tax and for social security tax if you are in a system with that coverage. You will pay tax on a portion of your retirement benefits (generally 75 to 90 percent), but will no longer be subject to social security tax unless you find other employment.

You also will pay tax on all other income except that from investments in tax-exempt funds. You will have to pay tax on part of your social security income if you exceed prescribed levels. The IRS instructions for preparing your Form 1040 shows how to compute tax liability on social security. The rules may well change from those which apply in the 1987 tax year, which currently taxes a portion of your benefits if your income level exceeds $32,000 for married couples and $25,000 for single persons.

The federal government now only permits you to claim an extra standard deduction of $600, if you are married, or $750, if you are single, for persons who are over age 65 or who are blind. These figures are indexed for inflation beginning in 1989. These deductions replace the extra personal exemptions repealed by the 1986 Tax Reform Act. For those persons who are both elderly and blind, two extra standard deductions are allowed.

State and local income taxes after your retirement will depend on where you live. Some states are more generous with their retired citizens than others.

All information relating to income taxation is subject to change. There may be nothing as certain as death and taxes, but don't be too sure about the taxes. Current dissatisfaction about the recent massive tax reform may well result in a new reality by the time you reach "D day."

Transportation

Your post retirement costs will drop only slightly so long as you rely on your own automobile for transportation. You will find you are driving fewer miles after retirement if you have been commuting long distances. Your car will last longer, your tires won't need replacement so often, and you may be able to find some reduction in insurance—those are the advantages. You will find that costs have increased even more rapidly than the reported increases in the cost of living when you do have to replace your car, buy new tires, have some repair work done.

When owning a vehicle becomes a luxury you can no longer afford, low cost transportation alternatives for persons over 65 are available. Many cities and towns have reduced fare structures on public transportation. Some cities have "dial-a-ride" taxi service, which provides door to door transportation for doctor visits, grocery shopping, theater attendance, and such needs at reduced cost.

Airlines have offered annual passes for persons over 65. These are of benefit only if you plan to fly frequently to a variety of destinations within the United States. There are restrictions on how many times you may fly to a particular destination. Amtrak also offers reductions for persons over 65. It has passes that permit you to take several trips within prescribed zones and time limits. The bus lines, such as Greyhound and Trailways, offer substantial savings for persons over 65.

Plane, train and bus fare reductions make it almost folly to think of undertaking long trips by private car. The convenience of public transportation becomes more attractive as you grow older even if you don't need the savings in transportation costs.

Medical Expenses

Post-retirement costs for medical expenses can increase drastically if you do not have Medicare coverage or some other hospital and physician insurance paid for by your employer or pension fund. Medicare health insurance for those not eligible for social security Medicare coverage costs $174 per month per person if you sign up for it at 65. Your cost will be a little less than that if your employer permits you to stay within your present group health insurance plan at your own expense. Those covered by Health Maintenance Organization (HMO) plans and who can continue that coverage after retirement probably will not need supplementary coverage. Those covered by Medicare will find it necessary to pay or be insured for the many costs not covered by Medicare.

Most health insurance does not cover eyeglasses, hearing aids, dentures, medicines, routine examinations or podiatric care. Few, if any, policies will cover custodial care for those not able to care for themselves but who do not need skilled nursing care. The macabre joke around convalescent hospitals is that you are better off if you have cancer than if you are senile.

These distressing costs of medical care rarely occur in the first 20 years of retirement. The early retirement years are usually trouble free. After 85, the human body seems to act much as an old car—repairs become more frequent and more costly. As you count down to retirement, you should include careful preparation for meeting these additional costs.

Insurance

You must know how to manage risk so that fate doesn't step in to wipe out your carefully laid plans. We often go blindly through life, vacillating between brinksmanship and super-caution. We either pretend that we live a charmed life or protect ourselves against every contingency, real or imagined. The optimists have too little protection against risk, the pessimists too much. Realistic pre-retirement insurance plans can help you to manage the potential risks.

Insurance is a commodity. Buy it as you would any other expensive item—very carefully. Your employer probably now provides you health and dental insurance as part of your fringe benefits. Make certain that you are able to retain coverage in the group after you retire if you are not eligible for Medicare benefits under social security.

Earlier we said our hypothetical friend, Mary Miller,

would receive no retirement income based upon her former husband's social security. Because she is eligible for spousal benefits, even though the entire amount is offset by her annuity from the state, she is still eligible for Medicare. This is an important factor for you who have no social security Medicare eligibility based upon your own social security. You may qualify under the spousal benefit rules if your spouse has social security coverage.

Life insurance should fit your needs, not those of the agent. Check out several reliable companies before you buy. Learn the advantages and disadvantages of various types of insurance: term insurance, straight life, limited payment life, and endowment. Life insurance may cost between one and 5 percent of your gross income. That is reason enough to exercise care in its purchase. There are several helpful sources of information listed in the Appendix to this book.

Auto insurance is not an optional expense if you own a car. It is mandatory in most states. As with life insurance, auto insurance should fit your needs. The law in your state on the coverage you must carry will control one part of your basic need. Beyond that you will need to consider coverage against collision, fire, theft and damage by uninsured motorists. After you have shopped carefully among reliable companies for the best coverage at the lowest price, you have one major way left to reduce your cost—consider the savings offered by raising your deductible amount.

Automobile insurance premiums are lower for those over 65 in many states. You may qualify for a further reduction in rates after retirement if you drive fewer miles because you no longer commute. Where you live could also affect your rates. You may find that the insurance rates drop if you relocate from an urban to a rural area. The complexity of rate structures for auto insurance is great enough to warrant seeking expert advice in the field. There are helpful sources of information listed in the Appendix.

Summary Of Basic Needs

Post-retirement expenditures will be less than pre-retirement expenses in terms of constant dollars in most areas. Even with inflation, for most couples, costs will remain within reach for many years to come. A single person, living alone now, however, will not notice substantial savings after leaving the work force.

In many instances income received during the first year of retirement will be greater than the take-home pay in the year before retirement. Add up your present deductions for income taxes, pension fund contributions, social security taxes, and tax sheltered annuity deductions. If these amounts equal approximately 35 percent of your current gross pay, you will understand why you will be able to live on a lower gross income after retirement than you need now.

You might consider working at a job during summer holidays that offers social security coverage if you are in one of the states where educators are not eligible for social security. The present law permits you to earn one quarter of coverage for each $410 you earn. You can earn no more than four quarters of coverage in any one year. The law requires 40 quarters for eligibility.

Beyond The Basics

Keep in mind the need to budget for entertainment, books and periodicals, travel and hobbies as you estimate your post-retirement expenses. These items are as important as the basic necessities, perhaps even more important. Retirement means that you will have time to enjoy life. You will not want to fill your days with dull activities undertaken to kill time.

How much will you need to satisfy your needs beyond the basics? That will depend upon what you want to do and how well you prepare for those activities while you are still working.

Are you interested in music or live theater? Plan now to become a volunteer usher. It may take a while to find an opening. Opportunities to hear concerts or to see plays free are in great demand. Once you are on the roster, you will be set for life or until your legs give out. The next time you go to a concert notice the person who shows you to your seat. Chances are it is a retired educator.

If you have talent and want to become a participant rather than a spectator, join your local little theater group. Be a spear carrier. It can lead to a lifelong adventure.

John S. taught accounting, but he really wanted to be part of the symphony orchestra. He did not play well enough to be a member of the orchestra, but he moonlighted for years as a member of the symphony stage crew. He had the satisfaction of involvement with "his symphony" that continued long after he retired.

A circulating library was born in one school's faculty room the day several staff members admitted they were swamped with the books they bought and the magazines they subscribed to. Why not reduce the cost and the clutter by exchanging books and magazines among the group? The idea flourished. There was a weekly exchange of reading material even after members of the group retired.

Hobbies can be self-supporting. Many hobbyists barter and swap materials. Others sell their services or products to support their hobbies. No matter what the hobby is, there is a group involved in it, ready to provide encouragement and activity. Attend any hobby fair and you will see evidence of support for fellow enthusiasts.

There are clubs, special interest groups, swap meets, seminars—all available at little or no cost.

Some who look forward to extensive travel after retirement fear that trips abroad will be too expensive. There are ways to cut travel costs, so there is no need to give up such dreams.

Colleges and universities all over the United States and Europe open their dormitories in vacation time to fellow educators, working or retired. Elderhostel, an organization devoted to life-long learning, publishes a catalog two or three times a year offering courses, board and lodging to people over 60. The organization offers courses at participating schools and colleges in the United States, the United Kingdom, Ireland, Germany and the Scandinavian countries. The costs are very reasonable.

There are international programs promoting travel by foreign teachers to the United States. The program seeks host families among American educators. The host families provide food, lodging and hospitality for two-week periods to guests from other countries. An enjoyable way to have friends in countries where you would like to travel is to become a host family for a few years.

Exchange students offer another way to establish lasting friendships with people from other places. The students come to look upon their host families as "other mothers, fathers, sisters and brothers." Their homes may become the "home away from home" for their host families.

Summary

How much should you plan to budget for expenses beyond the basics? Budget as much as you can. Remember research, investment of time and ingenuity often are as valuable as money. There is no reason why retired educators should forego the impossible dreams of their younger years.

Inflation

No matter how well you feel you have planned for retirement, if you have not faced the issue of inflation, you are not ready for the shock of shrinking dollars. Inflation, even at 2 percent a year, will nearly double your costs in 30 years. At an annual rate of 4 percent that doubling will occur in 18 years. To keep pace with the constant erosion of purchasing power, you should prepare to have income which grows with increases in the cost of living. Thirty years of retirement on a fixed income with 4 percent inflation could prove disastrous.

4 Taking Stock: How Much Will You Have?

Now that you have made a realistic estimate of how much income you will need to enjoy a satisfactory life after retirement, it is time to estimate how much income you can reasonably expect to generate.

Take stock now while there is still time in your countdown to retirement to make up any anticipated deficits.

Computing Retirement Income

The following chart will help you to organize information concerning your income at retirement. You may not expect to have income from all the sources listed. But these are the sources of most income streams for most educators after retirement.

Each entry will alert you to the possibility of income from that source. It is a good idea to make up separate charts for you and for your spouse.

Source	Monthly Amount
Teacher's retirement system	$_____
Social security benefits	$_____
Other retirement systems	$_____
a.	$_____
b.	$_____
c.	$_____
Tax deferred investments	$_____
Government bonds	$_____
Individual retirement accounts	$_____
Interest on savings, bonds, etc.	$_____
Withdrawals from mutual funds	$_____
Real estate rentals	$_____
Other sources	$_____
a.	$_____
b.	$_____
c.	$_____
Total monthly amount	$_____

Teacher's Retirement System

Are you covered by a state teacher's retirement system? If the answer to that question is yes, then your next question should be, "How much will I receive if I retire at age 55? At age 60?"

There is no uniformity among the 50 states regarding the answers to those questions. Some states base retirement benefits on a percentage of the average highest three years salary times years of service. Other states use different formulas. Many states change the percentage to reflect the age of the teacher at retirement.

Take the case of John D. who is now 40 and expects

41

to retire at 60 with 30 years of service. At age 60 in the state where John teaches, they pay 2 percent times years of service times the average of his highest three years' salary. John is now making $28,000. In the next 20 years, he can expect promotions and cost of living increases to bring him to a top three year average of $56,000. To compute his retirement benefit, he multiplies 2 percent times 30 years of service times $56,000. He finds he can expect to receive $33,600 per year.

If John feels that he wants to retire at age 55 with 25 years of service, he must first reduce his anticipated average top three years salary by about $6,000. To compute his retirement benefit he multiplies 1.4 percent times years of service times $50,000 and finds that he can expect to receive $17,500 per year. If John wants to retire early he must either reduce his anticipated standard of living at retirement or find a way to make up the substantial reduction that early retirement would cost him.

Your personnel office is the place to go to determine the rules which apply to you. Study the information you receive carefully. Are you in a system which permits you to receive credit for service in another state? Are you in a system integrated with social security? How does the formula for computing benefits change with age at retirement? Would you substantially improve your benefits by moving from the classroom to administration for the three years before retirement? All of the answers to these questions have a direct bearing on your retirement planning.

A word of warning before you write down the magic numbers: Read the fine print concerning options which will affect the amount you can expect to receive. Read the material in Chapter 6 regarding the effects of options which permit continuation of annuity benefits to a surviving dependent or spouse. Each of these options is critical to your retirement plan. Consider them carefully in light of all of your other possible retirement income. Your teacher's retirement system benefit is just one part of your total retirement income. You need to look at the total picture.

Social Security Benefits

If you are an educator in a state which includes teachers and other school employees in the social security system (a majority of states do), you should investigate the amount you may expect to receive from that source. Check your local telephone directory for the social security office nearest you. Ask them to mail you the latest information regarding social security benefits. Send a letter with your social security number, date of birth, name, address, and signature to the Social Security Administration in Baltimore, Maryland, 21203, for specific information regarding your social security account and an estimate of your prospective retirement annuity based upon current data.

Keep two things in mind when making projections regarding social security benefits. First, the actual amount of the benefit reflects cost of living increases from year to year. Hence a figure given this year will increase by the time you reach retirement age. Second, your benefit based upon your annual contribution increases with your annual covered income. As you earn more money, you earn a greater potential benefit. You should request information about your account periodically, so that you can update your estimated income at retirement. Your periodic update can serve to alert you to the need to find other sources of income to support you when you reach "D day."

Other Pensions

Many educators work in more than one retirement

system during their careers. Some work in both public and private elementary and secondary schools. Some teach in public school systems in more than one state. Others work in public and private universities or community colleges as well as K-12 systems.

Each of these systems or institutions has some pattern of retirement benefits. Those who left contributions on deposit in one system when moving to another find that they have retirement benefits from both. Because most systems assure a minimum benefit amount, the amount of your entitlement may be more than your total contribution. Those few years of service you put in outside your regular system may prove to be a welcome source of additional income.

Don't overlook any possibilities. When computing your potential retirement income, check with all previous employers to determine what benefits are due you because of membership in their systems. Your work-related retirement benefits from state teacher's retirement systems, social security and other pensions form the core of your retirement income.

Those benefits are subject to changes in laws relating to cost of living adjustments and taxation. However, they are not going to disappear with a shift in the economic winds. Your greatest danger is that those work-related pensions may shrink in purchasing power over your long years of retirement.

When you have added all of your work-related benefits and determined what that basic retirement is going to be, you may well see the need for additional income from other sources.

Tax Deferred Investments

Currently the federal government permits teachers to shelter up to approximately 20 percent of their income each year in either tax sheltered annuities or tax sheltered investment accounts. Under certain situations or circumstances, an increased percentage is permitted. Changes in the tax law in 1986 altered some ground rules, but the fact remains that tax deferred savings are a legal and helpful way for you to augment your retirement income.

Tax sheltered annuities are available primarily through insurance companies. Most school districts permit a range of choice among companies and plans. You make your selection of a plan and your employer deducts the amount you wish to save from your paycheck and deposits the amount into the tax sheltered annuity. At the end of the year your reportable gross income shows on your W-2 form not as your actual gross salary but as your actual gross minus your tax sheltered savings. You will not pay taxes on the sheltered savings until they come back to you as annuity payments after you retire.

Most tax sheltered annuity plans pay a specified amount of interest each year on your savings, interest which is also tax deferred. Some annuity plans invest your money in funds which pay variable rates of return. There is always the prospect that a variable annuity plan can earn more return than a fixed rate plan. The possibility also exists that such a plan could, in a bad year or period of poor management, fail to equal the interest guaranteed under the fixed rate plan.

Another type of tax sheltered investment account is available where the company invests your deposits as you direct in stocks, bonds, or mutual funds. You cannot withdraw the funds in such accounts without paying the deferred tax plus any penalties. You may shift your investment from stock to stock or from stocks to bonds or mutual funds. If you have the time and interest required to become knowledgeable about investments, such tax sheltered investment accounts can help you to add to your future retirement income. If you are unwilling to spend the time and effort required to invest wisely, you would probably do much better with a fixed rate tax sheltered annuity.

In any tax sheltered investment account you must take into consideration the cost of buying and selling securities. Before you make a choice of an investment account for your tax sheltered funds, you should talk to more than one broker. Find the firm which has the best track record on handling such accounts. Remember you must handle even a tax sheltered account wisely. You need to avoid the dangers of "buying high and selling low," of failing to buy quality, or of holding on to favorite stocks in spite of dismal performance.

To illustrate the possibilities of tax sheltered annuities, consider the experience of Sam and Susan S. He is a 40-year old science teacher. Sam has taught for 10 years and expects to teach for 20 more. He earns $32,000 a year now. Susan, his wife, is also a teacher. She has only recently returned to teaching after dropping out to raise their two boys who are now 13 and 15. Susan earns $20,000.

From their combined gross income of $52,000 Sam and Susan have a taxable income of $43,000. They decided to save $300 a month in a tax sheltered annuity. As they receive 10 paychecks a year, they will be putting $3,000 a year into their TSA. That $3,000 subtracted from their taxable income of $43,000 reduces it to $40,000. The reduction saves them $70 per month in federal income taxes and $20 per month in state income tax. They add the combined $90 per month tax savings to their TSA. This means that Susan and Sam are able to save $4,080 a year. If they never increase the amount saved per month in the 8.5 percent fixed interest rate annuity, at the end of 20 years they will have saved over $206,000. If they quit depositing when they retire at 60, but don't withdraw any funds from the annuity account until they reach 70, they will have over $465,000 to draw on to supplement their other retirement income. The amounts withdrawn at that time will be taxable as current income.

Government Bonds

Another form of tax deferred savings is available through investment in government series EE bonds. The amounts invested in such bonds are not deductible from gross income as in the case of tax sheltered annuities. The interest on the bonds, however, is not taxable as income until you cash the bonds. A thousand dollar face value bond costs $500. You must hold it until maturity to realize the face value. Interest accrues through periodic increases in redemption value and you receive it at the time you cash the bond.

Series EE bonds are best used to shelter interest on funds put aside for use before retirement. There isn't any penalty for cashing them before reaching age 59.5 as there is when withdrawing money from individual retirement accounts or tax sheltered annuities.

While the interest on EE bonds is subject to federal tax upon redemption, the interest is not subject to state or local income tax. To the extent that your income is subject to state or local income tax, you are securing tax exempt income from your series EE bonds. You cannot transfer, sell, or use these bonds as collateral. You must cash them to realize their value. You may purchase them in the names of minors and the increased value realized at redemption is taxable current income for the person named as owner.

Individual Retirement Accounts

In addition to tax sheltered annuities or accounts,

teachers are eligible in some cases to shelter funds in individual retirement accounts. The law now permits you to invest up to $2,000 per year for each employed spouse but sets up limits to govern the IRAs deductibility from current year gross income for federal tax purposes. Where there is only one employed spouse, the law limits the total amount to $2,250 per year for a couple filing a joint return.

Whether or not the IRA contribution is deductible, the interest earned in the investment still accumulates tax free until it is withdrawn. But because you and your wife probably are covered by a state teacher's retirement plan, there are other factors limiting your IRA's tax deductibility. Only if you and your spouse are not covered by a qualified pension plan do you retain full tax deductibility for your IRA contribution each year, no matter what your income level.

Single educators with an adjusted gross income of $25,000 or less, or a married couple filing jointly with $40,000 or less still may deduct the contribution even if covered by a teacher's retirement plan. Over those limits, the deduction is reduced until it is completely lost at $35,000 for a single teacher and $50,000 for a married couple filing jointly.

You may invest IRA savings in insurance annuities, bank, credit union or savings and loan accounts, mutual funds, money market funds or self directed brokerage accounts. Each of these investments carries advantages and disadvantages. Each has costs. Some are riskier than others. Those investment opportunities such as credit unions and bank savings accounts which entail very low risk also bring low rates of return. Where the possibility of greater return exists, the risk of loss is also higher.

In some states money invested in individual retirement accounts is not deductible from your gross income for state tax purposes if you have some other retirement plan.

Tax Exempt Investments

When you exhaust your ability to shelter savings from current taxation, there is another kind of investment which will permit your savings to grow without taxation, now or later. Investments in tax exempt securities are not tax deferred. The money you invest initially is not deductible from current income. The income from such investments is, with a few exceptions under current law, free of federal, state or local income taxes.

Tax exempt securities are bonds issued by state municipalities or political subdivisions. Tax exempt bonds usually carry much lower interest rates than other types of taxable securities. They fluctuate in value depending upon interest rate trends. If interest rates are going up, the value of a fixed rate bond will decrease. If you must sell such a bond, you may have to sell it for less than you paid for it. If, on the other hand, interest rates are falling, a tax exempt state or municipal bond with a good return may actually increase in market value. When you buy a state or municipal bond, you know that barring bankruptcy of the issuing agency you will:

a. Receive the face value of that bond when it matures, regardless of what you have paid for it; and

b. receive interest at the rate stated on the bond. The interest you receive is tax free income with one exception.

When you compute your income for purposes of determining whether you must pay federal tax on a portion of your social security income, you must include the interest you receive on tax exempt securities.

You can reduce the risk inherent in investment in tax

exempt securities in three ways. First, you can avoid purchase of any bonds rated by Moody's or Standard and Poor's at less than AAA. These business analyst firms publish ratings on credit worthiness of tax exempt issues which range from AAA down to C, with AAA the highest. A C-rated bond will pay a higher rate of return than a triple A bond, but the risk of a default is correspondingly higher. Second, you can buy bonds which carry insurance against default. There is a modest fee for the insurance. Third, you can spread your risk by purchasing shares of mutual funds based upon tax exempt securities.

Unlike the purchase of a specific bond with a fixed redemption value and rate of return, mutual fund shares based upon tax exempt securities will fluctuate in value and in rate of return. Some tax exempt mutual funds have performed very well over the years and have proven to be sound ways to accumulate additional retirement income. Other funds have not done so well. Never invest in a mutual fund without considerable investigation.

Remember there is no guarantee that future performance will equal past performance. Check not only the performance of a fund in comparison with other funds during the past years, but during weak and strong market periods.

Some fund managers turn in spectacular records in good times, but seem unable to cope with adversity. If you are buying shares periodically so that you are "dollar averaging" your investment, you can survive and even thrive when your fund shares decline in value.

However, if there is a possibility that you will want to sell shares in a hurry when values may be low, it is wise to avoid any mutual fund with a widely fluctuating price per share.

Stocks

When you pick up the morning paper and read that the stock market has reached another all-time high, the temptation to rush out to join the crowd of investors is very strong. Many market analysts will tell you that you should do just the opposite. Investing in the stock market is neither a certain way to fortune nor to bankruptcy. There is nothing as risky as investing on the advice of friends or acquaintances unless it is betting on a sure thing at a horse race.

If you want to invest in stocks, you should prepare to spend time and effort learning how to invest rather than to gamble. There are no perfect investments which bring you a high return with low risk. There are some investments which are better than others. It takes time, patience, and study to find quality stocks which will grow in value over the years and give you a fair return on your money.

One of the best ways to prepare yourself for active participation in the stock market is to join an investment club. Such clubs pool investors' money. They research alternatives before purchasing shares. Investment clubs share the costs of subscribing to market letters and other sources of information. Members learn to read financial statements and to judge when a company is well or badly managed. Members also learn to anticipate turns in the economy to avoid bandwagon purchases or panic sales. If your faculty doesn't already have its own investment club, you can form your own. Write to the National Association of Investment Clubs, 1515 E. Eleven Mile Road, Royal Oak, Michigan, 48067, for information.

In addition to joining an investment club, there are other ways to learn about stocks. The Bank of America publishes a book called *Understanding Financial Statements*. You can obtain it from any branch of the bank.

Your local library has copies of *Value Line Survey*, Standard and Poor's *Stock Reports*, *Barron's*, *Forbes*, *Financial World*, and *Wall Street Journal*. Studying each of these will add to your knowledge. The New York Stock Exchange publishes some basic educational pamphlets. You may obtain copies from local member firms such as Smith, Barney or even your local Sears Financial Center. Brokerage houses are in business to make commissions on sales of securities. They are eager to have you as a customer; therefore, they are more than willing to help you to understand the business of investing. One of the better introductions to the intricacies of the stock market is in Sylvia Porter's *New Money Book For The 80's*. The book not only gives you a guide to the stock market, it includes an extensive investment bibliography, as well.

Remember that the stock market, whether it is the New York Stock Exchange, the American Stock Exchange, or the over-the-counter market, is unpredictable. The market includes good investments and bad ones. Just because a firm has a familiar name, it does not necessarily represent the quality you want and need for investment of your hard earned money. Experts in the investment field have reported that in the preceeding 10.5 years before mid-1984, the average annual rate of return in real dollars (purchasing power—dividends plus price changes) for the 30 issues in the Dow Jones industrial stock index came to only 5 percent. That means that your savings would have grown in value by only a very modest amount. On the other hand, had you deposited your money in an ordinary pass book account 10 years ago, it would now be worth about half of its value in real dollar purchasing power.

The same risk of erosion of value takes place any time you lend money. You may say, "I never lend money," but you do all the time. Whenever you deposit money in a bank, savings and loan, or credit union you are lending that institution your money. Whenever you buy a corporate, federal government, or municipal bond, you are lending money to the issuer of the bond. Your strategy for enhancing your retirement income probably already includes lending money through the purchase of bonds. We have already discussed federal and municipal bonds. Now is the time for a brief review of corporate bonds.

Corporate Bonds

Corporations have two major ways to increase the money available to them for expansion, modernization, or simply for working capital. They can sell part ownership of the firm. They do this by issuing stock. On the other hand, they can borrow the funds they need. They do this by issuing bonds. Some bonds represent a mortgage on the fixed assets of the firm. These are the most secure because they represent a straightforward claim on the company's assets and earnings. Other bonds represent a second level of indebtedness called debenture bonds. These represent a claim on the corporation assets after satisfaction of mortgage bonds. A third kind of bond is the convertible debenture. You can convert such debentures into shares of common stock under specific conditions.

If the value of the common stock has risen to exceed the value of the convertible debenture and the specified conditions of conversion are present, you can shift from being a lender to being a part owner of the corporation. This is a benefit which you do not have with an ordinary mortgage bond or a straight debenture.

The advantages of corporate bonds are primarily safety and reliability of income. If you buy a 20-year, 10.5 percent bond which carries a triple A rating, you can be fairly certain that you will receive regular semi-annual payments at a rate of 10.5 percent per annum for the life of the bond. At maturity you will receive the face value. The disadvantages are a possible erosion of capital and diminuation of earnings. If you buy a 20-year, 6.5 percent bond at face value, say $10,000, you will lock yourself into that interest rate for the life of the bond even though during that 20-year period interest rates may have soared. The market value of your bond will be discounted if you are obliged to sell under such circumstances. The face value of $10,000 which you will receive at maturity will have substantially lower purchasing power than the $10,000 which you paid for the bond even at 2 or 3 percent per year inflation rates.

There is a way to invest in bonds which will protect you from some of the disadvantages without sacrificing the advantages of bond ownership. Buy mutual funds which are based on bonds. Let the professionals who understand the complexities of the bond market manage your money. This will not guarantee a reliable source of supplemental retirement income, but it will enhance the possibility that you will avoid making a costly mistake through ignorance.

Mutual Funds

No matter what kind of investment you fancy — stocks, bonds, commodities, tax exempts, foreign companies, growth, high yield, you name it—there is a mutual fund out there based upon that type of investment. Your problem, when deciding to purchase shares of a mutual fund, is to find the best managed fund with the best track record which meets your investment goals. Mutual fund shares represent part ownership in a portfolio of stocks, bonds, or commodities.

Your share value and dividend return depend on how

well the managers of the fund do their job of trading. Families of funds managed by one company permit you to make shifts among various types of funds as conditions change. This can be an advantage if your investment goals change from growth with its high risk to income with its lower possibility for incremental increases in value, for example.

Many investors have found mutual funds to be sound vehicles for month after month investment of fixed sums. Reinvestment of dividends, capital gain distributions, as well as dollar averaging the cost of shares combine to bring some educators to retirement with a substantial supplement to their teacher's retirement system, social security benefits and tax sheltered annuity accounts.

Those satisfied investors didn't achieve their goals blindly. They monitored the performance of their mutual funds. They consulted authorities in the field of mutual fund analysis such as Wiesenberger Financial Services, *Moody's Bank and Finance Manual, Forbes* magazine, *Donahue's Money Fund Report,* and the yearly *Consumer Reports* issue on mutual funds. All of these authorities are available in your local public library. If you have the misfortune to live in a community where the public library has an inadequate collection of financial publications, check the nearest larger public library or college library. Expenses incurred for trips made to gather investment information required to manage your portfolio of investments can only be used to offset other investment income.

You don't have to sell your accumulated shares in a mutual fund to realize an income from that fund. You can, after retirement, elect to receive the income from the fund in cash rather than reinvesting it. This gives you a continuing supplement to your pension income without eating into your capital.

You should be aware that all income from a mutual fund not part of your tax sheltered annuity or IRA plan is taxable in the year received. Those funds which stemmed from capital gains prior to 1986 tax law changes were taxed at specific rates. Since Jan. 1, 1987, such gains are treated as ordinary income.

Interest income is ordinary income for tax purposes. You will receive (and so will the IRS) a statement each year reporting the source and amount of your earnings. You will pay tax on those earnings even though you never actually see them because they are reinvested.

Real Estate

We indicated earlier that lending money was not the best way to accumulate wealth over the long term because of the effect of inflation on the principal. Polonius advised, "Neither a borrower nor a lender be." He may have been on the side of prudence with his admonition against lending, but what of borrowing? Is it possible to make money by taking on debt? At this writing, yes, particularly if you borrow money to purchase real estate. Most educators who spend most of their careers with one district or institution of higher education find it wise to purchase a home rather than to rent. No matter when you make your original purchase, you can expect that by the time you pay for your home, it will have increased in value. Some of the lucky generation who have experienced the remarkable inflation of real estate values during the 1970s already know that inflationary pressure can be a blessing in disguise. Tract homes purchased for $30,000 are in most communities selling for two to three times that amount. Even when taking the amounts paid for interest on the home loan into account, the money invested has not lost its purchasing power. Because the government feels that home ownership is a social good, property taxes and interest payments remain tax deductible amounts, saving the home owner hundreds of dollars in federal and state income taxes each year.

The increased value of the family home is available to the owner in several ways. An equity loan can provide additional dollars for investment. The reduction of taxable income by the amount of the interest on the loan, under certain specific conditions, will help meet the increased payments. The sale of the home and the purchase of a larger, more expensive dwelling may shelter all of the gain on the sale from taxation. If the owners choose to rent the property rather than selling it, they can secure the down payment for another home through an equity loan. The former home can then provide a source of additional income through write-offs available on rental property.

For those parents faced with the expense of providing housing away from home for sons or daughters attending college, purchase of a house or condominium in the college community can prove to be a sound investment. The child rents from the parent at market value and the dwelling for tax purposes becomes rental property. You can increase the return on the investment if the property has enough space for shared use by other students. The main drawback to this scheme stems from the higher cost of maintenance caused by student use. Those costs, fortunately, are tax deductible business expenses. After the children no longer need housing, you may either sell the dwelling or continue it in use as an income producing rental until such a time as it no longer provides tax benefits.

Will You Have Enough?

Now that you have taken stock of actual and potential sources of income available to you from pensions, annuities, and investments it is time to balance your books. You have estimated how much you will need. You have taken stock of your available resources. Now you need to develop a strategy for making up any deficit which you think will occur when you reach "D day." That is what a countdown to retirement is all about — *Planning*.

5 Having Enough: How To Prepare

Take time now to make up a budget, not as a strait-jacket spending plan but as a snapshot of your present situation. If you don't keep monthly expense records, don't worry. Go through your checkbook, your income tax return, your credit card statements and other records of expenditures. The data are there. When all else fails, you can always keep records for a few months.

While you are preparing your budget estimates for the basic necessities, pull together information on all of those budget categories listed by the Bureau of Labor Statistics [see Chapter 3]. Some of the categories, such as Transportation and Medical Expenses, will change when you retire. The former will go down, the latter will increase.

Income taxes also may decrease after retirement. Changes in the Tax Code made in 1986 may alter significantly your after-tax retirement income. An excellent book, *The Educator's Tax Planning Handbook*, published by United Resources Publishing, is available to you upon request. This work is devoted entirely to tax matters. It will guide you in your countdown to retirement.

The habit of keeping records is a good one to develop. A simple posting of expenditures each month as you pay your bills can be a treasure trove of information as data accumulate. You can build into your budget an early warning system to alert you when you have spent too much in a specific category.

Increased Savings

Decide now to put at the top of your budget the amount you want to save. Pay yourself first. Call it "delayed gratification," if it makes you feel less guilty about your selfishness. Your children will bless you later when you are financially independent in your retirement years. The decision to put savings first on your list of priorities will focus your attention on possible ways to economize.

Do-it-yourself skills are the key to more discretionary income both now and later. The cost of service is out-pacing inflation. The plumber, the painter, the handyman are all preparing for a retirement lifestyle you can only envy. The auto mechanic who services your car, the service station attendant who pumps your gas represent holes in your savings bucket. They are not the only ones. Make a list of everyone you pay to provide you a service. Ask yourself, "Could I do it myself?" If the answer is, "Yes, if you knew how," then learn how. Adult education classes are open to teachers as well as to other taxpayers. Don't be afraid to learn "Auto Shop," "Plumbing" or "Basic Dress Making," if those are skills you need and lack.

Don't be afraid to save money. You don't have to be

a miser, but you don't need to be the town philan-
thropist, either. Buy carefully, no matter how small the
purchase. Shop for groceries after dinner, not on the
way home when you are hungry. Pass up the eye-level
shelves. Look along the bottom shelves for the real
buys. Shop the perimeter of the store. That is where you
will find the food that is best for you. Check unit prices.
Resist the impulse to buy if you don't need the product.
Check local farmers' market prices against those of the
supermarket. Buy when produce is fresher and
cheaper directly from the producer. Know prices before
you stop at a roadside stand. The poor but honest
farmer may not always be either.

Prepared foods are a trap for the unwary. Check the
cost of packaged soups, rice, pasta, TV dinners, cake
mixes and sauces. Look at the list of ingredients on the
label. Could you duplicate the food at a lower cost with
a modest amount of effort? If so, buy the necessary
materials and add the difference in cost to your savings
account. There are excellent cook books which guide
you in the preparation of your own pre-mixed foods.
You can find copies of such books in your public
library. Browse through the back issues of *Consumer
Reports*, the magazine published by Consumers Union.
In many issues you will find recipes for making your
own pre-prepared foods.

Consumer Reports is also an excellent source of information on buying the highest quality products at the
lowest cost. The magazine provides in-depth coverage
on everything from appliances to zoom lenses. Other
periodicals such as *Changing Times*, *Money*, and *Sylvia
Porter's Personal Finance* magazines also contain information on cost-effective consumer expenditures.

Your goal is to spend your money wisely. Anything
less than that will decrease the amount of money you
can save between now and retirement. Look again at

that list of budget categories. One which represents a significant percentage of your budget is clothing. Every working man and woman has to budget substantial amounts for apparel worn on the job. Educators are no exception.

Purchase clothing that is quality merchandise with classic styling at the end of the season. Those clothes will not only be bargains, they will last more than one year. Prepare for wardrobe replenishment by checking your present garments, shoes and accessories. Determine what colors and styles will compliment those clothes you already have and want to keep. Throw out your mistakes. Make a list of what you really need. The orange alligator bag marked down to $10 may be the most expensive purchase you will ever make if you must buy an entire wardrobe to go with it.

There are many discount and factory outlet stores throughout the country where you can find quality merchandise at near wholesale prices. Fall River Mills, Massachusetts, and Flemington, New Jersey, are two towns with nationwide reputations as "bargain hunters' paradises." There are factory outlets in almost every major city.

Have you checked the Junior League thrift shops for Saturday clothes? The folks on the hill buy high quality garments. They donate them early to their favorite charity. Again, don't permit a fancy label to influence you if you wouldn't want anyone to see you in the garment, even in your own back yard. A Pendleton shirt received for Christmas or birthday which was too large or too small could find its way unworn to the thrift shop. Look for the rare finds. You will have fun browsing through the shop even if you don't find something every time you go. The funds raised support very worthy causes.

Nobody who likes to read should pass up a Friends

of the Library book sale. Donate your personal library discards. Buy those books you have always wanted to read but not to keep. Your purchases will make it possible for the library to improve its services. That is truly a worthy cause.

As you examine your pattern of expenditures, you will find places where you can save money without diminishing the quality of life now. Penny-pinching which deprives you of those things which make life bearable is neither desirable nor recommended. You are looking for waste, for leaks which contribute to neither your present nor to your post-retirement well-being. You are looking for lazy dollars which you can put to work earning additional income.

Even with the best of intentions, it is sometimes impossible to save money on the salaries paid many educators. Teachers salaries are still falling behind increases in the cost-of-living. If there is no money to save, you have at least three alternative ways to increase your present income. First, you can invest money in yourself. Second, you may augment your salary by moonlighting, by finding part-time employment. Or you may earn the extra money you need by creating your own business—self-employment.

Invest In Yourself

You can have more money when you retire if you increase your annual income during your working years. The formulas used by most retirement systems guarantee that those in higher income brackets before retirement will be in higher income brackets after retirement.

Look at the salary schedule in your district or institution of higher education. The ordinary classroom teacher or lecturer is customarily the lowest paid. Salaries increase with seniority but not as fast as with promotions. Work your way up the career ladder by investing in your own potential. If one of the paths to promotion depends upon more education, secure those degrees or certificates. If you can earn more money as a master teacher, develop the skills required for that position. Learn to play the games of promotion politics. Keep in mind those future years of leisure. They will be more enjoyable if you have no financial worries.

Part-Time Employment

It is unrealistic to expect most educators to find time during the school term to take on employment beyond their regular jobs. Single parents, particularly, are already working at teaching and maintaining their households. To suggest that they take on additional employment is to suggest the impossible. However, there are those rare times during the summer holiday periods and in the years after the children leave home when you can fit a second job into your schedule. Working in a field related to your teaching specialty is helpful both financially and educationally. The social science teacher who works in a state or local government job during the summer, returns to the classroom better prepared to make the study of government relevant to current problems. The history teacher who works in a museum, or an archeological dig, or as a research assistant in a library, returns to the classroom better prepared to make history interesting. University professors who work as consultants, who become part of the world their students will soon join, are in a better position to transmit useful knowledge. An elementary school teacher who works with a welfare department, a pre-school, or a child abuse prevention group during the summer vacation learns as well as earns. No educator loses by investing time in the world beyond the groves of academe. During school hours you see the public faces of your students and their parents. During the summer when you are working in a position that strips you of your authoritarian role, you are more apt to see their private faces, the social, economic, and emotional problems that shape their behavior.

It is as important to prepare yourself for part-time employment as it is to prepare yourself for retirement. Make a list of the skills you have to offer a prospective employer. Make a list of the values which will obtain from each job you seek in terms of benefit to students. When you apply for a position, let the person hiring you know what you will bring to the job and what your employment now will mean to the quality of future entry level employees.

If you can't find the part-time employment you want, it is time to consider self-employment.

Self Employment

Do you have a special skill, a hobby with commercial possibilities, expertise in an area where there is a need to be filled? Are you a risk taker? Do you have the patience to start on a modest scale and nurture a business to the point where it will provide a satisfactory return? Do you know what limits the law puts upon conducting a business enterprise from your home? Are you aware of the hazards of buying franchises? Do you know the advantages and disadvantages of joining with others in partnerships?

These are but a few of the areas you should explore before you undertake the roller-coaster ride known as entrepreneurship. It is easier to become self-employed by selling services than by selling products. The initial investment is smaller and you limit the chance of loss. On the other hand, the fantastic successes of the men who started Apple Computers, who created Hewlett-Packard, and who gave birth to similar firms in garages or spare rooms can be very tempting. For every David Packard, there are hundreds now making their way through the bankruptcy courts. If you can stand the heat, the kitchen may be just the place for you.

With those words of caution in mind, we can explore some of the possibilities and advantages of self-employment for educators.

Self-employment, even when practiced on a part-time basis, provides some tax advantages through business-related deductions. Check with your accountant or tax preparer to assure that you know what the legal deductions are and what records you must keep to support your claims.

Self-employment can mean that you qualify for commercial rates when you travel, for wholesale discounts when you buy supplies, for sheltering additional retirement funds under Keogh retirement plans.

A useful guide to the advantages of self-employment is *The Self Employed Teacher* published by Teachers Tax Service, 1303 E. Balboa Blvd., Newport Beach, CA, 92661. Additional information may be gleaned from periodicals such as *Money*, *Women's Day*, and *Sylvia Porter's Personal Finance* magazine.

The most familiar areas for self-employment for educators are those related to teaching, such as tutoring, private lessons, coaching or child care. These can be lucrative enterprises because they call for very low overhead. You are selling your knowledge. Less often thought of but in the same low overhead category are writing, lecturing, consulting and development of classroom teaching materials.

Nancy N. teaches kindergarten. She has, over the years, been increasingly concerned about children coming to school not ready to learn. She put together a guide to things parents could do between a child's birth and entry into kindergarten to assure that the youngster came to school advantaged, ready to learn. Nancy used the guide as the basis for a series of classes for new parents. She sent a letter to each family listed under new births in the local paper offering the classes at a modest fee. She also posted notices on bulletin boards in hospitals, supermarkets, and laundromats. She soon found that she had more demand for her classes than she could handle. Her expenses were low and her profits added a substantial amount to her income. Nancy found after a few years that she had made her kindergarten teaching job easier and more effective.

Bill W. teaches in high school. His field is science. In his youth he had been a champion swimmer and diver. He made an arrangement with a local health club to use its facilities to give private swimming instruction to children of members. The arrangement is mutually beneficial to Bill and to the club —to Bill because he receives fees for his lessons and to the club because Bill's swimming champions attract new family memberships.

John P. teaches French. Every year he takes adults and high school students to France for a six weeks total immersion in the language and culture of the country. John's charge for the program covers not only his transportation and living expenses but a fee for his services as well.

Other educators prefer to take a break from teaching. They find self-employment in other fields.

Howard C. does landscape gardening. Andrew M. restores old houses. Betty W. does wallpapering and interior painting. Helen P. does auto repairing. Each is earning extra income. Each is finding enjoyment providing a service far removed from students and classrooms. More daring are those who take the risks of establishing small businesses which they carry on in their free time or through employees. Whether it is a music store, a small appliance repair shop, or a fast food outlet these educators are learning through trial and error skills that they can use after retirement. While they are learning they are, if they have done their homework, earning extra income to augment their current salaries and to put aside for retirement.

Not every self-employed educator wins in this risky game, but most insist the knowledge they gain of how business operates is worth the losses they chance.

Your goal is preparation for retirement. Having enough money is an important part of that preparation but it is not the only part. Planning for change is equally important.

6 Cover All Bases: Plan Ahead

So far this book has dealt with the sunny side of pre-retirement planning. You've seen that you can, with proper financial strategy, have enough money to enjoy your years of freedom. Now is the time to consider the cloudy days, the days when you no longer have a spouse to share financial burdens with you.

You will be tempted to skip this chapter. Please don't. This chapter contains information vital to your countdown to retirement. Authorities in the field of financial planning have a rule which you should keep in mind. The rule is: Don't make financial decisions when you are *mad, glad,* or *sad.*

If you are in the midst of a divorce, don't give everything away just to be free.

If you are in love with the most wonderful person in the world, don't make decisions you could regret when ardor cools.

If you are bereaved, don't let your grief decide your

plans for the future.

Financial Planning

The time to do financial planning, to anticipate change in status, is now while you are in a period of calm.

It is a hard fact that one spouse is going to die before the other. Simultaneous death is so rare as to be statistically insignificant. In view of those facts, it is folly to put off until tomorrow preparation for the time when you must manage alone.

There are three things you must consider. First, you must consider planning for financial security during the years alone. Second, you must consider writing a will to control the disposition of your estate. Third, you must consider giving someone you trust power of attorney to handle your financial affairs if you are incapacitated.

Financial Security

What happens to your financial status when your spouse dies? There is little doubt that it will change. Your future income will depend upon how well you prepare now. The role of the impoverished gentle-woman may seem romantic in a Victorian novel, but in reality living below the poverty line is pure misery. You and your spouse will want, before you make irrevocable decisions concerning retirement benefit plan options, to weigh carefully what those decisions will mean in terms of financial security for the survivor. It is very easy to go to extremes, either sacrificing survivor benefits for present enhancement of income, or sacri-ficing a considerable portion of income you could enjoy together to increase the survivor benefit.

Ken H., a school administrator in California, was 65 when he retired. His wife, Anita, was 60. She retired from her secretarial position with city government at the same time her husband retired. In Ken's family, males were noted for their longevity. Since Ken felt that he would live as long as his wife, he chose an unmodified retirement plan which gave him 60 percent of his final salary. Anita also took an unmodified retirement plan. These decisions gave them maximum income for their retirement. Unfortunately, Ken died in an automobile accident three years after they retired. Upon Ken's death, Anita's income decreased by $2,250 per month.

Joe P. taught English at a secondary school, also in California. When he retired, he knew he was in ill health. He, therefore, took the option which provided that upon the death of either himself or his wife, the state would pay one-half of his modified monthly allowance to the survivor. Joe lived 20 years after retirement. His wife lived only two years longer. They were protected against the severe loss of income suffered by Anita H., but they were obliged to forfeit a considerable amount of comfort to pay for that protection.

Neither extreme is wise. Where both spouses are working and contributing to savings, there is mutual interest in resolving these matters to maximize benefits for each of them. You should resolve problems through mutual effort with professional help.

This is one time you should not "do-it-yourself." You should engage the services of an attorney and/or a financial planner — one who specializes in working with educators. Decisions made now will have serious consequences if they are not legally or financially sound.

Once you have chosen your counselor and made an appointment to discuss financial planning, ask what you should bring to your first meeting. Keep in mind that attorneys and accountants charge by the hour. Their rates are usually much higher than the hourly rates of educators; so, go prepared. Don't waste their time or your money.

Make certain that you have given careful thought to your goals. It is your plan and it must fit your needs now and be amenable to change as your needs change.

Don't be timid about expressing your desires. Too many couples feel that such planning indicates a lack of trust. Be assured that it does not. Joint planning to protect those you care about is affirmation of your love.

Changes In Income

No matter how carefully you plan there will be some changes in the amount of income available to meet needs. Most pension plans permit reduction in the primary benefit during the lifetime of the annuitant. This insures that a percentage of the benefit will continue throughout the life of the surviving spouse, as we saw in the case of Joe P. Few plans, if any, continue payment to the survivor at the full amount of the primary annuity.

If both spouses were receiving social security payments based upon their individual eligibility in addition to teacher's retirement system benefits, the social security payment to the deceased spouse will stop. Social Security Administration rules state that a spousal benefit going to a surviving spouse must be offset by two-thirds of any government pension received by that person. In effect, that means that if the surviving spouse receives a teacher's retirement system annuity of more than the social security benefit, there would be little or no social security payment because of the offset rule.

To illustrate how this works, we will look at two families, the Shorts and the Hunts.

Shorts*—Both covered by an integrated social security (SS) and teacher's retirement system plan (TRS).

	Income at Retirement		Income after Frank's death	
	SS	TRS	SS	TRS
Frank	$ 700	$1500	$ 0	$ 0
Ellen	600	1000	600	1000
Total	$1300	$2500	$600	$1000

Ellen had social security benefits based upon her own earnings, hence the offset rule did not affect her. She had no social security survivor benefits. Because both she and Frank took unmodified annuities, Ellen had no continuing payment from Frank's teacher's retirement system benefit.

Hunts*—Clyde covered by private pension (PP) and social security (SS). Grace covered by teacher's retirement (TRS), no social security.

	Income at Retirement			Income after Clyde's death		
	PP	SS	TRS	PP	SS	TRS
Clyde	$800	$700	$ 0	$ 0	$ 0	$ 0
Grace	0	110	360	400	460	360
Total	$800	$810	$360	$400	$460	$360

Grace received at retirement one-half of Clyde's social security offset by two-thirds of her government pension. After Clyde's death, Grace received one-half of Clyde's private industry pension. She was 65 at the time of Clyde's death. She received 100 percent of his social security benefit ($700) offset by two-thirds of her teacher's annuity ($240), netting $460.

The examples given above are for illustrative purposes only. You should check your retirement system for options available and the consequences of selecting each modification. Decreases in survivor income might

---

* Names changed to protect privacy

be mitigated by payments from life insurance carried by the deceased spouse.

You should purchase such insurance policies at least 10 years before the date of your retirement to qualify for the lower premium rates. (Companies base rates on the age of the covered individual at the time of purchase and rates increase significantly after age 50.) You should discuss the purchase of insurance with a professional financial planner rather than an insurance or annuities salesperson.

Other Annuities

The balance left in an Individual Retirement Account goes to the heirs of the deceased owner of the account. If the beneficiary continues to receive installment payments, his or her life expectancy controls the terms.

Michael H. and his wife each had IRA savings of $7000 at the time they retired at 65. They started drawing out of Michael's account at the rate of 1/14th per year based upon his life expectancy. They drew out of Bonnie's account at the rate of 1/19th per year based upon her life expectancy. When Michael died at age 72, Bonnie continued to withdraw funds from his account at the rate of 1/13th per year based upon her life expectancy.

Some Costs Will Increase

What happens to your expenditures when your spouse dies?

Income taxes will go up. If your spouse was over 65, you will lose those extra exemptions which formerly helped to shelter some of your income. If your spouse was not yet 65, you will lose one exemption and will have to file as a single person. You will not qualify as head of a household unless you have someone dependent upon you for support. These changes in your filing status may be offset by the reductions in income discussed above.

Household costs will go up. Food for one person costs more than half that of food for two. You will find that you will again spend more on convenience foods, because cooking for one is no fun. You will find that many tasks previously done by your spouse will be beyond your capacity to perform. You will have to hire someone to do those chores as long as you continue to live alone.

The economic burden of maintaining your residence will seem to be heavier, even if it is not. The costs of heating and cooling are as much for one as for two. The costs of property taxes, painting, and repairs are just as much for one as for two. The pressure to find smaller quarters to reduce those costs will be great.

Don't make a decision to move for a year, or even two. Wait until the shock of the loss has diminished. You built your support network around your familiar neighborhood. Relocation means losing those friends. Even shopping in a new supermarket can be a traumatic experience when you are already under stress. Don't move in with one of your children or even move to be near them unless you are no longer able to care for yourself. When one parent dies, children see the other parent as suddenly very vulnerable, even though you may still feel quite capable of managing your own affairs. Here is the best kept secret in the world: The body ages, the mind does not. Your body may be 80 but inside of that body you are still 30 or even 18. Don't permit well meaning friends or relatives to make you old before your time.

You can continue to have a financially secure retirement if you have planned your financial strategy well. You, however, will be responsible for yourself and to your heirs. You must make or remake your will so that the estate you have created will go to whom you want to have it.

Wills

Next to your birth certificate, your marriage license and your professional credentials, your will is the most important document you possess. Properly drawn by an attorney, your will speaks for you when you are no longer here to speak for yourself. It puts into motion your intentions backed by the full force of law. Your will can cause family feuds as bitter, if not as deadly, as that of the Hatfields and the McCoys if it is not properly drawn.

The state will distribute your hard-earned money for you if you die without a will. The state legislative body dictates the terms of the distribution in the Probate Code. Those legislators who drew up the probate laws didn't know that you were closer to your step-children than to your sister. They didn't know that you had always promised your china to a favorite niece. Only you know those things. Your wishes can be declared null and void if you fail to put them into writing, properly signed and witnessed.

Don't wait until you retire to have an attorney draw up your will. A well-written will can protect your spouse and your children. If circumstances change, you can and should revise your will.

What you put in your will is up to you. Some things are permissive, others are mandatory.

If you have particular desires about burial or cremation, state them.

If you have an aged parent or a minor child who must be cared for, you should designate the individual you wish to have appointed to act as guardian. In the case of your minor children, if they have a natural parent surviving you, the court may not permit such a designation. If you have been divorced and do not want the court to appoint the children's surviving natural parent as guardian, discuss the matter with your attorney. If the court awarded you full custody, take that document with you when you go to have your will drawn.

You must name an executor of your will. You may state that person may serve without bond.

You, of course, will provide for the distribution of that property which is yours to dispose of. Take with you, when you see your attorney, copies of deeds to real property, ownership certificates for any automobiles or boats you may own, insurance policies, records of savings accounts, and investments. All of these records will tell the attorney what you may dispose of under your will. You should identify specific bequests of real estate, stocks or bonds held in your name as your sole and separate property. You should also identify bequests of real or personal property that is yours by gift or inheritance. Willing "mother's china to my oldest daughter" won't do if there is more than one china set which might possibly have come from mother and if there could be a question of whether you meant the oldest or the oldest living daughter.

Your signature on your will must be witnessed by the number of persons required by law in your state. Witnesses should not be beneficiaries under the will. It is advisable that witnesses not be persons so old that they could be long dead when your will is probated. These witnesses should be within reach of the court in the event the probate judge requires them to attest to your signature or state of mind when the will was drawn.

The tax implications of bequests to your spouse are matters best left to the attorney drawing your will. Federal estate tax laws are now very generous and few educators will have estates large enough to tax under present limits. Laws could change; so proceed with caution.

Leave your signed will with your attorney, but take a copy or copies with you. Keep one copy in your home and let your executor know where it is. Place a second copy in your safe deposit box. In case you want to change your will, make certain that you destroy the original and all copies of the old will.

While you are meeting with your attorney on the matter of your will, ask about drawing up a power of attorney giving a person of your choice power to act in your name.

Power Of Attorney

It may seem strange to read that it is wise to give someone else power to sign checks and other papers for you. It is, nevertheless, a wise move, particularly if you are a single parent or you have lost your spouse.

You may limit the power granted to a specific time or to a specific deed. Even with limitations, granting such a power to an institution or an individual is not something you do without exercising caution.

Selecting a trusted relative is better than choosing a stock broker or a real estate agent. After retirement, if you plan extended travel, it is wise to grant power of attorney to someone who will take care of your affairs while you are away. Discuss the granting of such power with your attorney and follow his advice.

Summary

Your countdown to retirement is incomplete without attention to three vital matters.

First, you should prepare for the time when you, alone, are responsible for all those matters you formerly shared with your spouse. That means consulting with a professional financial planner specializing in educators and putting your affairs in order. You and your spouse should both know where you keep all important documents. You should both know what investments you have and where you deposit money. Both of you should know who carries your life, home and auto insurance. You each should be able to carry on the financial direction of your estate without the other.

Second, you and your spouse should each have a will properly drawn by legal counsel and witnessed. These wills should be on file in your attorney's office with copies in your home and in your safe deposit box. Your executor should know where you file your will.

Third, you and your spouse should give a trusted person power of attorney to act for you under conditions suggested by your legal counsel.

Once you take care of these matters you are ready to consider how you will protect your family against the catastrophic consequences of illness.

7 Wellness

Your health probably will improve once you leave the classroom or office. You will escape daily exposure to every flu and cold epidemic going around. Nevertheless, continuing good health is not that easy. You need to think about "an ounce of prevention."

NASA scientists monitor the health of each crew member as part of the countdown procedure prior to lift-off of the space shuttle. They do not want to have some person fail during the mission.

Your mission is to live a vigorous, alert, undiminished, unimpaired life right to the last day of your lifespan. You want nothing to interfere with the successful accomplishment of that goal. When you are no longer restrained by having to work for a living, you want not just to fly, but to soar. Wellness is your space shuttle. During your countdown to retirement and afterward, you should monitor your lifestyle and your environment to prevent illness or injury.

You are as old as you feel. Nobody was ever compelled to enter a nursing home because he or she couldn't run a marathon or swim 40 laps. It is the ability to undertake the activities of daily life that keeps an older person independent.

Areas significantly related to health problems are fitness and exercise, nutrition, safe and proper use of medicine, accident prevention, and prevention of substance abuse. These are all areas within your individual ability to control.

You aren't going develop brittle bones because you were exposed to a virus. You will develop brittle bones (osteoporosis) if you have not had appropriate preventive treatment.

You aren't going to develop clogged arteries because you have reached your 65th birthday. You will risk developing cardiovascular problems if you enjoy too many sirloin steaks and rich desserts.

You won't find it suddenly difficult to walk upstairs, because you have retired. You will risk reduced mobility problems if you sit long hours a day and fail to maintain physical fitness through exercise.

What can you do to prevent illness and to maintain independence?

Don't Just Sit There

"If exercise could be packaged into a pill it would be the most widely prescribed and beneficial medicine in the nation." So said Robert N. Butler, M.D., former director of the National Institute on Aging.

Unfortunately for all of us, we cannot package exercise as a pill to take while we read a book or watch television. Exercise requires effort on the part of the individual.

You don't have to enroll in a program or find a team to join to enjoy the benefits of a regular exercise program. Walking at a brisk pace for 40 minutes to an hour a day is as good as "an apple a day" for keeping the doctor away. Heart specialists and other health professionals often tell their patients, "Walk three miles a day." If your area has safe bicycle trails, you might prefer to bicycle. So long as you do it regularly and vigorously, it serves the purpose. Those who are afraid to bicycle or walk out-of-doors need not forego the exercise. There are stationary bicycles and treadmills available at reasonable prices.

Of course, you can find more exciting ways to assure physical fitness. If you prefer tennis or golf, play regularly. If you want company while acquiring physical fitness, join your local YM/WCA. If you prefer to join a health club, be an informed consumer. Don't fall victim to high fees, false promises, and/or companies which will soon go out of business.

You can have fun and maintain fitness, flexibility, balance and coordination. Swimming, bowling, jogging, aerobic dancing and square dancing are all good forms of exercise.

If you don't have the exercise habit, now is the time to start. Exercise is not just for kids.

A word of warning. Don't try to compete with a teenager and don't try a marathon the first day out. Moderation until you have developed stamina is the best way to insure that you will be able to keep going. Walk before you run.

You should also fuel your body with proper nutrition.

We Are What We Eat

Many of the chronic diseases which take much of the fun out of retirement have their roots in either malnutrition or chronic over-nutrition. You don't have to be a starving resident of Ethiopia to suffer from malnutrition. Many well-educated, financially well-off persons are malnourished because they are afraid to eat certain foods, they are trying to lose weight, or they rely on fast foods or junk foods to satisfy their nutritional needs.

A sensible diet is not difficult to maintain. You will be neither malnourished nor overnourished if you eat in moderation a diet rich in fresh vegetables, fruits, low-fat dairy products, beans, fish, lean meats and whole grains. You should avoid fats, excessive salt, sugar, and alcoholic beverages.

Some authorities believe that as we grow older we should take a one-a-day vitamin and mineral pill to supplement our diet. They feel this is an insurance against vitamin and/or mineral deficiency. They all warn, however, that excessive use of megavitamins, fad diets, bran or other fiber products can be counter-productive.

You should check with your doctor about the advisability of taking vitamin D and calcium. Some doctors advise women to supplement calcium treatment with some form of estrogen. You can help avoid the problem of osteoporosis with a combination of diet and exercise, provided they are undertaken before onset of the disability.

A broken hip can be fatal under certain circumstances. It can be very annoying in others. Avoiding brittle bones is far better than heroic measures to overcome their incapacitating consequences.

Hypertension and diabetes are two other health problems which can be alleviated by proper nutritional practices instead of extensive medication. Don't rely on medicine to bail you out after years of chronic malnutrition or over-nutrition. Becoming a "pill-popper" can be hazardous to your health.

Wise Use Of Medicine
Every educator knows that the solution to a problem

can often cause more problems. The same is true of medicine.

We are in an era of wonder drugs. Do you have arthritis? Take a pill. Do you have high blood pressure? Take a pill. Are you constipated? Take a pill. Are you depressed? Take a pill. Have a cold? Take a pill.

Look in your medicine chest. You will find bottle after bottle of prescription and non-prescription drugs. Taken wisely according to your doctor's directions, those medications should cure you. What a new doctor or specialist doesn't know about your medical history when he is prescribing a new medication could make you very ill. The medicine could even kill you if that medication reacts adversely with other medicine that you are already taking.

Be aware that reactions to drugs can vary according to the age of the patient. Medicine taken with no side-effects at 30 may, because of impaired liver or kidney functions, be dangerous to an 80-year-old.

Some drugs can lead to mental confusion in the elderly and to a false diagnosis of senility. Many older persons confined to intermediate care facilities are victims of well-intentioned medication.

When you visit your physician let him know before he writes your prescription:

What other medications you are taking.

What reactions you get from certain types of medicine.

What allergies you have.

Ask whether you should avoid certain foods when taking a new medicine. Ask when you should take the medicine. Should you take it before or after meals, before bedtime, first thing in the morning? Ask about possible side effects from the medicine.

Don't wait for the doctor to tell you or ask you about these matters. You should not be intimidated because he is a professional. You are a professional, too. It is your health that is your primary concern. You don't want an accident to shorten your life span.

Accidents Seldom Just Happen

Bizarre accidents kill many people. Children die of burns because tap water was too hot. Adults electrocute themselves with electrical appliances in the kitchen or bath. Older people die of falls down stairs or in the tub or shower. Freak automobile accidents kill scores of people.

Each of these so called accidents was preventable, but someone neglected to take proper precautions.

During your countdown to retirement you need to sharpen your awareness of potential hazards around your home. The life you save, as the old saying goes, may be your own.

A brief checklist of potential hazards and a periodic inspection to make certain that you are living in a relatively safe environment can go a long way toward preventing an accident from "just happening."

Summary

All of the persons mentioned in Chapter 1 who are enjoying their freedom from the world-of-work have one thing in common—good health. That good health was not achieved by good fortune or good genetic inheritance alone. Each of them prepared for an active retirement by paying attention to the factors which contribute to wellness.

Wellness means more than the absence of disease. It means being physically fit, properly nourished, and free from injuries caused by preventable accidents.

Wellness is your key to a vigorous, alert, undiminished, unimpaired life right to the last day of your lifespan.

Wellness is less expensive in the long run than illness. It is worth the time and effort you put into it now and for the rest of your life.

There are times, however, when illness or injury is unavoidable. When those times occur after retirement you should know how to protect yourself from catastrophic financial consequences.

Medicare

Medicare comes in two parts.

Persons over 65 are entitled to Part A hospital insurance. It is free for those covered by social security. If you are one of the few who are not eligible for Medicare Part A without charge, you may elect to buy that coverage by signing up for it as you are nearing 65 and paying the required monthly premium.

Part B is optional medical insurance for which everyone enrolled pays a premium. The government adjusts the premium annually in line with cost of living adjustments to social security benefits. You don't need to be eligible for social security to qualify for Medicare Part B. If you wish to enroll, do so as you are nearing your 65th birthday. There is a 10 percent per year penalty for enrollment after you reach 65.

To enroll in Medicare, you need to visit your local social security office at least three months before your 65th birthday. Take proof of age with you when you go to apply.

If you think you have just discovered that free lunch which everyone says doesn't exist, you are wrong. Medicare does not provide you with complete coverage for all of your medical needs. In actual experience, Medicare covers about half of your medical expenses.

Part A (Hospital)

Medicare Part A does not cover the full cost of hos-

pital confinement. Your coverage has a several hundred dollar deductible for each benefit period. A benefit
period begins the first day of hospital or skilled nursing
facility confinement. It ends when you have gone 60
days without being admitted to either type of facility.

If your stay in the hospital is longer than 60 days, you
will have to pay a portion per day toward your hospital
bill for the next 30 days of confinement. After the 91st
day, you have a choice of paying the full cost yourself,
or drawing on your 60 lifetime reserve days. You must
pay all costs if you do not draw on the 60-day reserve.
You will need to pay a larger sum per day toward your
hospital costs any time you use one of the reserve days.

Most periods of hospital confinement are of less than
60 days duration. Patients are most often discharged
during the first 30 days. You have two options open to
you if you still need skilled nursing care at the time of
discharge from the hospital. You may transfer to a
skilled nursing care facility or choose to have home
care. In either case the physician must authorize
skilled nursing care or therapy before Medicare will
provide coverage.

You will pay a fraction of the cost for the first 20 days
of confinement in a skilled nursing facility. You will pay
a larger fraction of the cost per day for the 21st through
the 100th day of confinement. You will pay full costs
after the 100th day.

You may have "covered home care" if you choose to
return home instead of going to a skilled nursing
facility. Home care provides part-time skilled nursing
care, therapy, and the services of home health aides.
The program has no limitation on the number of visits
or number of days and you pay nothing.

Again, if you think that this last option will take care
of you at no cost during your declining years, you are
wrong. Your doctor must prescribe skilled nursing

and/or therapy services. You do not qualify for benefits if you simply need help to dress, eat, bathe, or go to the bathroom. Nor do you qualify for these services if you have not first been in a hospital for three days.

The home health care services are a better choice than a skilled nursing facility if you have a family member able to give you supplemental intermediate or custodial care. The skilled nursing care is for a very few hours out of the day and night.

You would need to supplement home health care if your convalescent period is prolonged. You must pay the entire cost of providing family members' relief from 24 hours duty day after day. Medicare will cover the full cost of services to a terminally ill patient in a Medicare qualified hospice. A terminally ill person is one who has six months or less to live. You must make a 5 percent co-payment for drugs, biologicals and respite care provided during a hospice stay.

Medicare Part B (Physician)

Medicare Part B helps to pay for doctor's services. That word helps is very important in your understanding of Part B coverage.

The medical carrier in your area decides the basis for the "reasonable charge" which you pay for covered services. "Reasonable charge" means the customary fee charged by most physicians for that particular treatment. Some doctors charge more than the Medicare definition of "reasonable." You must pay the first $75 of reasonable charges each year, then Part B will pay 80 percent of the reasonable charges. That does not mean that part B is going to pay 80 percent of your medical bills. Doctors are free to charge as much above the "reasonable charge" as they wish.

You will pay only the remaining 20 percent if you have a doctor who will accept the "reasonable charge" as his fee. Part B coverage includes outpatient services as well as hospital visits and services; physical, speech and occupational therapy; and an unlimited number of skilled home health care visits each year. It also covers medically necessary ambulance transportation to or from a hospital or skilled nursing facility and other outpatient services and equipment. All of these services are subject to the 80/20 sharing of "reasonable charge" noted above. As with Part A, Part B leaves many gaps in your coverage.

"Medigap" Insurance

Insurance companies often refer to policies designed to cover the gaps in Medicare coverage as medigap or co-insurance policies. By whatever name, they are policies designed to supplement Medicare coverage. Policies, as a rule, do not extend coverage beyond that provided by Medicare. Such policies usually pay the $400 deductible in Part A, the additional costs per day for hospital stays between the 31st and 150th days, the $75 deductible for Part B plus 20 percent of "reasonable charges."

Co-insurance rarely covers the cost of hospital days beyond the 150th (or the 20th day in a skilled nursing facility). Such policies do not cover doctor's fees beyond Medicare established "reasonable charges."

Buying more than one co-insurance or medigap policy is often a waste of money. Policies rarely provide duplicate coverage. One of the worst kinds of consumer fraud is the selling of medigap policies to frightened older persons when they already have adequate coverage. In some cases, people have as many as 10 worthless policies, purchased because of false promises and scare tactics on the part of fly-by-night salesmen.

Medigap policies rarely cover services not covered by Medicare. Excluded services include hearing aids, eyeglasses, dental services, and podiatric care. There are exceptions to this generalized rule regarding services covered. You will find a wider variety of covered services offered by many Health Maintenance Organizations' (HMOs) health insurance policies.

HMOs

Health Maintenance Organizations (HMOs) offer health services to their members covering both outpatient and hospital care. When you join an HMO you are buying not only care when you are ill but preventive services as well.

The advantage of selecting an HMO scheme for your health insurance coverage is that you are not paying under a "fee for services" arrangement. It is to the benefit of the HMO to prevent you from having a serious or costly illness because you pay the same prepaid monthly amount, sick or well.

These organizations usually ask that you come in for periodic physical examinations and visits with your physician. They keep your medical records in a centralized file. Each physician, specialist or other person serving you knows your medical history, what illnesses you have had, what medicines you are taking, and what the results of your latest X-rays, EKGs, or other tests were. In this respect the HMO is much like the old fashioned family doctor who did not have to ask for your medical history each time you saw him.

The best of the HMOs offer classes in self-care which they encourage members to take. They help you to quit smoking and to break other health-impairing habits because it reduces profits for the HMO if you become ill. Better HMOs provide unlimited hospital days and doctor visits at no or very low charge. They provide low cost prescription service, eyeglasses, and other prosthetic devices.

The disadvantage of the HMO, in the minds of many, is that you may choose as your personal physician only doctors on the organization staff. In a smaller HMO that choice may be such that you can't find any doctor whom you like. In larger organizations your range of choice is greater. The criticism that you never see the same doctor twice is valid if the HMO does not permit you to select your doctor from among staff members. In most Health Maintenance Organizations, they prefer that you do make such a selection. Your choice, and your satisfaction with that choice, helps the organization to know when a staff member is rendering satisfactory service.

Another criticism of HMOs is that they frequently use "physician assistants" rather than physicians to perform routine health appraisals, and similar health services. They do, indeed, make every effort to be keep costs low, within the limits of good health care.

The cost of belonging to a full service HMO is about the same as buying Part A and Part B of Medicare if you are not eligible for social security.

You should check out the Health Maintenance Organizations, both in your present location and in the area that you have chosen for your retirement home, while you are making plans for retirement.

Care Of The Fragile Elderly

Why, in your countdown to retirement, would you need to know about care for the fragile elderly? You have years to go, even after retirement, before you will reach the point where you will need such care. There are two reasons why such information is important to your retirement planning.

First, you may have parents or aging relatives who are your responsibility and who might very well need care of this type just as you are about to retire. As lifespans increase, many retired individuals are finding that they have aged parents to care for just when they can least afford those costs.

Second, you should have some idea of what life-time care communities charge and what alternatives are available.

As we mentioned in the discussion of Medicare benefits, Medicare does not cover custodial care. You may have to provide at your expense intermediate care for your aged parent or other relative who is too fragile to stay alone. You may arrange this by hiring a full time housekeeper or taking the individual into your own home. Neither solution is without problems.

The alternative to those solutions is a retirement home or an intermediate care facility.

Retirement homes are of two kinds.

First there is the type where you pay a monthly fee for a room, apartment, or cottage. Included in the regular monthly charge are accommodations, three meals a day, laundry, weekly cleaning service and all utilities except telephone. Such retirement homes are for older persons who are still mobile and need no assistance. They provide a secure environment with a full range of recreational activities. In general, they equip living quarters with call buttons for emergency use. They take the resident to a hospital or skilled nursing facility if he or she needs medical attention. Rent continues as long as the furnishings of the resident remain in the room or apartment. Rates for retirement homes vary. The range is from $500 to over $2,000 per month, depending upon the area, the amenities, and the size of the living quarters.

In sum, this type of retirement home is for active older persons who want to be free of all problems of maintaining a home and who value companionship of others of their age group. Churches, fraternal organizations, and non-profit as well as for-profit corporations operate such homes.

You should weigh the advantages and disadvantages carefully before you decide on long-term residence in a retirement home. Eating in the same hotel-type dining room for the rest of your life could become very boring. The retirement home activities director might well drive you mad. Almost all homes pride themselves on the full range of activities available, activities in which they feel you should participate . Going to a retirement home is much like going to a summer camp, only the stay lasts all year-round.

A second type of retirement home is a life-care community. You must be in good health when you apply for admission. Life-care facilities will not consider your application if you already need either skilled nursing or custodial care. In these communities you pay a set fee upon admission and a monthly fee thereafter. The admission fees are high. Some charge as little as $80,000, others ask that you sign over all of your assets. For these admission fees and monthly charges (which run about the same as those of retirement homes) you receive lifetime care. You will have no worries about future hospitalization, skilled nursing care, or custodial care. They are all included in the charges. Most of the communities guarantee that they will care for you even if you cannot meet the full monthly fee.

The waiting lists for admission to retirement communities is long. Some require months of waiting, others require years.

The advantages are similar to those of retirement homes plus the guarantee of lifetime care regardless of the state of your health. The disadvantage is that once you have paid your admission fee and have passed the limited period when they permit you to change your mind, you are, figuratively speaking, locked in for life. The quality of care might change. Management might change. Nevertheless, you can't change your residence without suffering substantial financial loss.

If you are considering either a retirement home or a lifetime care community, you will find them listed in your telephone directory. You may contact your church, teachers' union, or fraternal organization for names of places they sponsor. Call and ask for brochures. Visit those place which are within your price range. Talk to some of the residents about the home or community. Look for the number of grumpy people sitting around, bored and unhappy. Contrast those with the number of happy, busy people bustling about. You will know which type of residence you prefer, if you do, indeed, prefer either.

Home Care Schemes

For those older persons who prefer to live independently, there is one other alternative to institutional care if they become ill. Many local communities offer homemaker services or in-home supportive services. These services are available upon referral from physicians, hospitals, or convalescent facilities. They range from homemaker services to professional nursing care.

The purpose of the homemaker services is to keep individuals out of institutions and in their own homes as long as possible. The charges for these services are in keeping with prevailing rates in the community. The advantage of utilizing such services over hiring through a domestic service agency or newspaper advertisement is that the persons providing the service are employees of the homemaker services agency.

The agency trains its employees to provide the type of service required. Unfortunately, these services, while less expensive than institutional care, often rapidly erode savings because your insurance does not cover them.

Insurance

Few companies write health insurance policies which cover intermediate or custodial care. If such coverage is of interest to you, you should check with a reputable, independent insurance broker in your area.

Summary

The best insurance against illness is prevention. Emphasis on wellness is better than facing the consequences of ill health.

Nevertheless, when illness strikes, you can ameliorate the catastrophic financial consequences through health insurance, Medicare, or membership in a Health Maintenance Organization.

There are many options for care of the single individual who doesn't want to live alone and the fragile elderly who can't live independently. These options range from retirement homes for active seniors to home care services provided through non-profit agencies associated with local service agencies or senior citizen centers.

8 Social Aspects

As we mentioned earlier when discussing problems which arise upon the death of a spouse, a support network is essential to your ability to cope with stress. Sometimes that stress is caused by retirement itself. At other times stress may be due to a death in the family, the act of relocating, or divorce. Whatever the cause, you need someone or some organization to be there for you, to help you weather the storm.

We rarely realize, as we work and live for many years in the same place, how much we come to rely on colleagues, neighbors, and familiar services to provide us with that network of support. When we change jobs or retire, we break links in the network, links which are essential to our psychological well-being. It is important in your countdown to retirement to recognize the need to provide significant alternatives to the links in this support chain that you will be breaking.

Social Ties

Loren C. was the superintendent of schools in an urban community. He and his wife, Debra, enjoyed a rich and varied social life. It was difficult for them to fit in all of the invitations to social activities which were extended to them. They in turn entertained the political and social leaders of the community in their home.

They normally made numerous out-of-town trips to conferences and conventions. All of these activities were in addition to the school functions they were obliged to attend. They had a warm circle of professional colleagues with whom they played tennis and golf.

Then Loren retired. The invitations went to the new superintendent. They could no longer travel to conferences or conventions at district expense. The professional colleagues who were not yet retired were too busy with school activities to play golf or tennis midweek. There was a great void where there had once been a full social life.

The couple had planned well for financial security. They had reached retirement in excellent health. Nevertheless, they had neglected to develop a circle of friends beyond those connected with Loren's position.

Your social life may not be of the same level as that of Loren and his wife. You could, nonetheless, find that you, too, will notice a void where you once had a round of enjoyable activities closely linked to your job.

How do you prepare for the day when old ties will be severed? Recognition that you and the colleagues you work with will have diverse interests after you retire is the first step.

The second step is to make an effort to develop close friends now in your neighborhood, church, or in organizations that you belong to which are not work related. Those friends will have the same tie to you after you retire as they do now. You will have common interests to hold you together.

The third step you can take before you retire is to participate in community affairs other than education. For example, visit your local senior citizens center. Discover what services you can perform to enrich the lives of those who have already retired who may not have the advantages you presently enjoy. Become acquainted with others who are volunteering their services. You and they have something to offer those individuals who come to the centers to learn new skills, or to extend their circle of friends. While you are sharing some of your knowledge and your time, you will be making new friends.

You will be learning how to cope with retirement. Giving of yourself before you retire builds a solid foundation for post-retirement activities.

The fourth step that you can take before you retire to build alternatives to your present social network is to establish a friendly relationship with your family. Now that your children are adults, you can stop being a parent and become a friend. Develop a relationship based upon mutual interests in a hobby or sport rather than on family ties. Forget trying to guide the younger generation. You have spent years as an educator and as a parent doing just that; now accept them for what they are. Permit your children to establish their own homes and their own families. Permit them to make their own mistakes. You may not approve of the way your grandchildren are being raised. Remember, your parents and your spouse's parents didn't approve your child rearing practices, either, and you muddled through somehow to get here today.

When you discard the role of nurturing parent, you will find your children are wonderful companions. You will find them a pleasure to visit and to travel with. As with all friends, remember to give them space in which to live their own lives. When you do get together, bring along laughter. It will make you feel younger and will ensure your welcome.

Of course, in some families this kind of friendly relationship between parent and child may be impossible to establish. Some families experience devastating disruptions caused by rebellion, drugs, and unacceptable behavior. In these cases it is far better to establish relationships with non-family members based upon mutual interests than to chance additional unhappiness by opening old wounds.

These steps are best taken during your countdown to retirement when you are taking them voluntarily, not because you are in desperate need to repair your social network.

It isn't enough to just make certain that you still have a social network to sustain you after retirement. Certainly the most important source of assistance for you in times of stress is your family and close friends.

Beyond that are sources of assistance which include fellow members of your church, professional and fraternal organizations. Beyond that source you will find many community organizations available to provide supportive services. Finally, many governmental agencies are available to help you.

Other Links In The Support Network

Whether your local teachers' organization is affiliated with the National Education Association or the American Federation of Teachers or neither of those national groups, there is a place for you after retirement. Both the NEA and the AFT maintain programs for retired educators which keep you in touch with other professionals. The programs of both organizations provide opportunities for you to remain active in your profession, to continue to work for social and educational issues important to you. They also provide top-quality insurance programs, discount purchasing opportunities, travel programs, information concerning second career opportunities and interesting avocations.

The NEA and the AFT both provide pre-retirement materials to help you with your retirement planning.

If your local teachers' organization is not affiliated with a national group, you are eligible to join the National Retired Teachers Association, which is now a part of the American Association of Retired Persons.

The AARP/NRTA publishes the NRTA *News Bulletin* and the NRTA edition of *Modern Maturity* magazine. Member services include a purchase privilege program offering discounts at major car rental companies, hotel and motel chains. Some of these discounts are quite generous. Marriott Hotels and Resorts, for example, offer a 50 percent discount on rooms at participating locations. Membership also gives you access to a pharmacy service providing a mail order service for low cost prescription and non-prescription drugs; a travel service; group health, auto, and home owners insurance; and an investment program.

National Retired Teachers Association in conjunction with the American Association of Retired Persons also provides the following services and programs, according to its information:

• **Consumer Affairs Program**: Helps older people become more knowledgeable consumers of goods and services. "Consumer Sense," a quarterly report, is available free.

• **Criminal Justice Services**: Offers programs to help older persons reduce or remove opportunity for victimization and understand the operation of the criminal justice system.

• **Energy Conservation Program**: Entitled "At Home With Energy," the program includes slide show, manuals and publicity posters. Information on organizing a community-wide conservation program is also included.

• **Health Advocacy Services**: Provides information about preventive health care, nutrition and chronic diseases. Program volunteers also teach older consumers how to use the Medicare system and the health care marketplace to their best advantage.

• **Housing Program**: Offers information and advice on many housing-related matters to individuals and groups. Encourages involvement in local housing programs. Serves as liaison with other private organizations and government agencies concerned with housing for the elderly.

• **Institute Of Lifetime Learning**: Enhances opportunities for older persons to continue their education by working with the academic community to establish local educational programs and provide a wide range of educational materials. It also seeks new initiatives for employment of older workers.

• **Legal Counsel For The Elderly**: Staff of legal and paralegal volunteers provides legal advice to elderly residents of Washington, D.C., especially in the area of public benefits. Technical assistance also provided in certain states with similar programs. Project is funded by the Administration on Aging, Legal Services Corporation and the District of Columbia.

• **Senior Community Service Employment Program**: Trains economically disadvantaged older persons and helps place them in permanent jobs. Funded by the U.S. Labor Department, the program now has offices in more than 100 sites in 33 states and Puerto Rico.

• **Tax Aide Program**: Helps hundreds of thousands

101

of older Americans prepare their tax forms each year. This free public service uses volunteer tax counselors trained by AARP in cooperation with the Internal Revenue Service.

• **Widowed Persons Service**: Provides organizational and training resources to local groups interested in community wide programs to serve newly-widowed persons. Local services may include volunteer outreach, telephone referral, group meetings, public education, and a resource directory.

You can contact the National Education Association by writing to them at 1201 Sixteenth Street N.W., Washington, D.C., 20036. The American Federation of Teachers can be reached by writing to them at 555 New Jersey Avenue N.W., Washington, D.C., 20001. The address of the National Retired Teachers Association is 1909 K Street N.W., Washington, D.C., 20049.

With all these services available to guide you in your pre-retirement planning and your post-retirement living, you have a truly extensive support network available through your profession.

In addition to these programs offered by professional educational organizations, your state and/or county government probably has a Commission on Aging which offers support services to persons over 65 years of age.

The federal government provides services though several agencies.

• **Administration On Aging**
Office of Human Development Services
U.S. Department of Health
and Human Services
330 Independence Ave. S.W.
Washington, D.C. 20201
This agency is responsible for programs authorized

under the federal Older Americans Act.
* **Health Care Financing Administration**
  330 C Street S.W.
  Washington, D.C. 20201

This agency has oversight of the Medicare program and has quality assurance responsibility over providers of health care services and the long-term care program for the aged, chronically ill and nursing home affairs.
* **Office Of Special Adviser For Elderly Housing**
  Office of the Deputy Undersecretary for
    Inter-governmental Relations
  Department of Housing
    and Urban Development
  451 Seventh Street S.W.
  Washington, D.C., 20410

This office is responsible for programs concerned with housing needs and fair housing opportunities.
* **National Institute On Aging**
  900 Rockville Pike
  Bethesda, MD 20205

The goal of the institute is to improve the quality of life by prolonging the productive middle years.
* **Social Security Administration**
  6401 Security Blvd.
  Baltimore, MD 21235

The SSA administers all facets of the of the social security program. It maintains the records concerning your contributions and compute benefits. It also has information concerning disability and death benefits.
* **Veterans Administration**
  810 Vermont Avenue N.W.
  Washington, D.C., 20420

The VA administers laws authorizing benefits for former members of the Armed Forces and their dependants. It has a comprehensive medical program involving a system of nursing homes, clinics, and medical centers.

Summary

You see, you are not alone. You do have a safety net of supportive services available to you to help you to cope with almost any problem you may encounter in your retirement years.

The National Education Association, the American Federation of Teachers and the National Retired Teachers Association all have programs to assist retired educators.

In addition, stimulated by such legislation as the Older Americans Act, there are local, state and federal agencies established to provide information and assistance to persons over 65.

One of the problems of greatest concern to older Americans is the problem of crimes against the elderly. These crimes include both assaults on your property and on your person.

Crimes Against The Elderly

The fear of crime is almost as disabling as the aftermath of a mugging, robbery or any other crime against your person or property. In actual numbers, retired persons probably suffer no more incidents of crime than the remainder of the population. What makes the fear of crime against the elderly so stressful is the knowledge that cases listed on the police records as minor crimes often represent major catastrophes to elderly victims. A purse snatching incident may result in a fall, a broken hip and death within a few months. A mugging may be the forerunner of intense trauma. A burglary may trigger irrational fear of repetition of the crime.

Persons who have lived outgoing, happy, independent lives often lose all interest in life after becoming victims of crime. How do you prevent becoming a victim of crime against your person or property? Even more important, how do you avoid becoming a victim of fear?

Law enforcement authorities are almost unanimous in their advice. They have a rule concerning protection against "con artists" which is simple, direct, and to the point. The rule is: If the offer appears too good to be true, it probably is.

You may never encounter a con artist who practices such threadbare scams as the "pigeon drop" or the "bank examiner." On the other hand, you may meet more sophisticated operators who practice less well publicized ways to separate you from your money. Operating through newspaper, television, or magazine advertisements, they offer such schemes as charity rackets, health clubs, medical quackery, missing heirs, pyramid schemes, referral sales, work-at-home and other money making opportunities. No matter how legitimate the offer may appear, don't part with your money until you have investigated thoroughly.

More serious than these petty swindles is the growing number of fake financial planners. While security dealers, real estate brokers, accountants and attorneys all require licensing, almost anyone can go into business as a financial planner. The phony financial planner promises high-yielding investments known only to a few insiders. The bait of extraordinary return is usually enough to encourage persons seeking financial advice to withdraw large sums from bank accounts or other safe, but low-paying investments, and hand it over. Then they find they are victims of a swindler. Fortunately, most financial planners are ethical and honest.

How can you assure yourself that the financial planner you have selected is honest?

In the first place, the con artist posing as a financial planner is more apt to select you as his mark than to wait for you to select him. A letter or telephone call promising unusual gain is often the first step in a swindle. Investigate all such offers with a securities broker, real estate broker, attorney, or accountant before you invest any money.

If you are searching for a financial planner who is honest and ethical, you should look for someone who:

Has been in business at least five years;

Is willing to give you references;

Is not linked to a single investment opportunity;

Has a proven track record with others in your financial range;

Will offer you a range of options to choose among;

Does not suggest that you put all your money into one investment.

Some simple rules will help to keep you from joining the growing list of those burned by incompetents or con artists masquerading as financial planners:

Make certain that your portfolio is characterized by quality, value and flexibility.

Do your homework. Know something about the companies you invest in.

Don't risk your retirement savings. If you want to take a risk, use money from current income.

Beware of fads, tax shelters, and unusually high returns.

Remember, if you expect something for nothing, nothing is what you will get.

Finally, if, after due caution, you feel that you have been victimized by a clever swindle, report the facts to the police. Failure to report a crime is to encourage the victimization of others. You need only suspect that something illegal is going on. Leave it to the police to investigate. Your job is to be aware. Their job is to apprehend criminals.

The same advice goes for other crimes as well.

The best protection you can have against street crime is not a whistle, not a can of mace, not a lethal weapon, but your own common sense. If you appear alert and in control you will not look like an easy victim. Muggers and purse snatchers are looking for situations which promise two things, ease of accomplishment and escape. Anything you can do to thwart either condition helps to protect you from attack.

Persons who walk in an alert and purposeful manner, checking beside and behind themselves occasionally, rarely encounter the street criminal. If they do, they are ready to give up their money without a struggle because they are not carrying more than they can afford to lose.

The best protection you can have against car theft or home burglary is, again, common sense.

A key left in the ignition is an open invitation to car theft. An unlocked car is almost as easy to steal as one left with the engine running. Packages or valuable clothing left in open view in a car are like a house key under the welcome mat.

A house left unlocked while you work in the yard, a window left open at night, a house key left under the door mat, a note pinned to the door telling what time you will return, all mark targets of opportunity for the person intent upon burglary. On the other hand, a lighted house with sounds of activity is unattractive to the criminal. A barking dog is not the burglars best friend.

A neighborhood watch program has cut house burglary rates significantly. In many neighborhoods, residents concerned about the safety of their persons and property have agreed to keep an eye on each others' homes and report unusual or suspicious activity.

Emily F. lived in a nice, middle class neighborhood where neighbors prided themselves on their disinterest in the affairs of others. There was not an eyebrow raised the day the moving van pulled up to Emily's house while she was away for the weekend. The only comment heard that day was praise for the speed with which the movers completed their work. When Emily returned to her empty house on Sunday evening, her next door neighbor was astonished to see her. "I thought you moved," he said. "We saw the moving van here yesterday." Emily's neighborhood now has a neighborhood watch program and not a leaf rustles without some attention being paid. A stranger is as closely watched as the proverbial pedestrian in Beverly Hills. There have been no burglaries in that neighborhood since the establishment of the neighborhood watch program. Word seems to have spread that someone is taking down license numbers of unfamiliar vehicles and reporting suspicious activity to the police.

If you feel that the urban area in which you live is unsafe, you may be tempted to take one of two radical measures to protect yourself. You may feel that you need the protection of a handgun, or you may feel that it is necessary to sell your home and move to a safer area.

Handguns are lethal weapons. In the hands of an novice, they are worse than no protection at all. If you feel that you need a handgun for family protection and you live in an area where possession of a handgun is legal, check with a reputable gun dealer for the names of organizations which provide training in the use of handguns. Learn what kind of weapon is best for you. Learn not only how, but when, to use that weapon. Learn and obey the rules for keeping a handgun in your home. There are too many innocent children and adults killed by weapons purchased for protection. Too many well-intentioned, frightened individuals find themselves embroiled in courts of law because they used lethal force in the wrong place, at the wrong time, or for the wrong reason. If you are unwilling to take the trouble to train, study and obey the laws about the use of firearms, don't consider the purchase of even "a little tiny" pistol.

The second radical option you may consider is relocation to a safer area. That option, in addition to the problems of severing ties to an established support network, has within it seeds of another kind of crime. You wouldn't buy the Brooklyn Bridge, but you might be astounded by the number of persons who buy swampland in Florida, desert land in Arizona, or inaccessible land in California sight unseen. Before you buy that dream property, check it out. If it is away from urban amenities, what is the cost of obtaining electrical and telephone service? What are the local zoning restrictions covering the property? Is the property large enough for an adequate septic tank system? How deep must you drill to secure an adequate year-round supply of potable water? Is the property subject to flood, earthquakes, or fire? What police and fire protection will you have?

Bill and Betty S. lived in a large, crime-ridden, midwestern city. When Bill was ready to retire from his position with the local school district, they decided to flee the city and to live in a mild climate in some area remote from civilization. They found a catalog offering properties throughout the Sun Belt states. They chose a beautiful site in the coastal mountains of Northern California. The price was reasonable and the company assured them that water, electricity, and telephone were all available.

With their deed in hand, Bill and Betty journeyed

west. After traveling through spectacular scenery, they reached the small town nearest their property. They stopped to ask directions at the local general store. They ignored the raised eyebrows and the lack of enthusiasm for their new home. They followed directions up a dirt road until they encountered a locked gate. Leaving their car, they climbed over the gate and proceeded on foot up the narrow trail through the forest until they reached what they believed to be their property. As they left the trail and walked a few feet into the brush, a shot rang out. The bullet hit Bill in the leg.

Hours later Bill and Betty reached the small town where they had started earlier in the day. They secured medical help for Bill and were told that the marijuana growers of the area took a dim view of strangers. Their dream of escape from urban crime was shattered, their hundred acres of mountain property was surrounded by an armed camp.

When they were finally able to reach the property, they found that it was not at all as represented. They learned the hard way that getting out of a bad real estate deal can be almost as costly as getting in. The next time they investigated before they purchased.

Bill and Betty aren't the only disillusioned purchasers of real property. Retirees receive many offers too good to refuse.

Offers of free vacations tied to resort area property sales abound. There are numerous time-share deals advertised by direct mail solicitation. Many magazines and newspapers carry advertisements for condominiums in Florida, Hawaii, Arizona, or Southern California. Life-care retirement home investment opportunities follow soon after a news story announcing retirement. Many of these offers are legitimate. Many are fraudulent attempts to persuade you to sell your valuable home and to invest the proceeds in some real estate scheme or another. Don't join the ranks of the disappointed. Use common sense. Don't rush into some purchase offered by a high pressure salesman. Legitimate real estate deals are available. They are waiting for buyers willing to do their homework, willing to investigate, to compare, to ask hard questions, to seek legal advice before signing purchase agreements.

Summary

Common sense and awareness are better protection against crime than expensive alarm systems or lethal weapons, according to many authorities.

To protect yourself against the con artist or swindler, the American Association of Retired Persons offers five sensible rules:

• Always investigate before investing money or signing a contract.

• Be suspicious about extraordinary promises of high or unusual returns, or a "bargain" no one else can match

• Don't discuss personal finances or give cash to strangers.

• Don't be too embarrassed to report that you have been swindled or victimized.

• Be willing to testify in court to help stop this kind of crime.

Older citizens do not need to lock themselves into their homes, prisoners of fear, if they are part of a caring community of neighbors. If no one else has started a neighborhood watch program in your neighborhood, start one yourself. You may find that your neighbors will welcome your concern for the safety of their persons and property. Your home represents a substantial investment. It may well be your most valuable asset. Do not sell it or exchange it for some other piece of property or investment without careful investigation.

III
Retirement

9 *Free At Last*

When you are in your early or mid-50s, there may come a morning when you will waken with a sense of dread and apprehension. A black cloud called education will envelop you. You will wonder if you can face another year in your present position. You will mentally replay the stresses of the past 20 years. You will remember the unmotivated students, the uncertainty of accomplishment, the low pay, the lack of respect. You will be tempted to say to yourself, "I can't go back. Life is running out. Teaching (or administration) is not worth the effort." If this happens to you, know that you are not alone.

Stress And Burnout

Throughout the United States there are thousands of educational professionals suffering the same symptoms of stress and burnout. About half of the teachers in this country plan to teach only until they are eligible

115

for retirement. Before you feel guilty about your loss of commitment to your profession, look at the factors which contribute to stress and burnout.

Dorothy Smith and Mike Milstein, authors of "Stress And Teachers: Old Wine In New Bottles," *Urban Education* (April, 1984), tell us that stress is not a new phenomenon. It has troubled educators throughout the 20th century. Smith and Milstein quote an article that Robert H. Snow wrote in the 1960s in which he pinpointed one of the principal causes of burnout. "There is no dependable means for the teacher to trace the consequences of teaching. If a rifleman on a rifle range were blindfolded and denied information as to where his shots were striking the target, his marksmanship would not improve," Snow had written. When you combine this lack of reinforcement of intellectual competence with ambiguity about the true role of the educator, it is no wonder that educators are frustrated and confused. Smith and Milstein conclude that if school systems won't change the environmental factors which lead to burnout and continue to place the onus for change on teachers, retirement or job change will continue to be a frequent response.

The California Commission on the Teaching Profession reported recently:

"There is reason to believe...that teachers in many schools face some or all of the following conditions: a deteriorating physical plant; inadequate quantities and quality of teaching supplies; excessive workloads (large classes, too many courses to prepare for, too many students overall); too many nonprofessional responsibilities, too many distractions and interruptions of class; and too little time during the day for planning and consulting with colleagues.... In most schools, teachers work in isolation and engage infrequently with other teachers on matters of the school's curriculum or institutional programs."

If this all sounds distressingly similar to a description of your situation, it is no wonder there is no joy in the prospect of another school year.

Henrietta Schwartz, dean of the school of education, San Francisco State University, states that a job must provide security, status and sociability. Schwartz defines security as encompassing freedom from fear, economic competence and intellectual success. She says that status includes self-esteem, social worth and career mobility. Sociability covers compatibility, friendship and productive interaction. Analyze your work experience over the past several years. If you find that these factors are no longer present, then it is time to consider early retirement or a change of career before you become physically damaged by stress and burnout.

During your countdown to retirement you have been careful to arrange your financial affairs so you will have sufficient resources to support yourself during your years of freedom. You have taken steps to attain and maintain good health.

Don't risk losing the game by stretching your years of employment past the time when you become aware of the symptoms of burnout. When you begin to be aware of feelings of helplessness, hopelessness, frustration, failure, lack of energy and purpose, then it is time to stop and take stock of your options. These symptoms are real. They stem from real causes. And they can be the forerunner of real illness.

You need a reprieve. You need some new stimuli. You need to consider early retirement, a career change, or both, for your own well-being.

Golden Handshake
It is only during times of teacher surplus or need to

reduce staff that school districts and institutions of higher education encourage teachers and administrators to consider the advantages of early retirement programs. They give programs names such as "Golden Handshake" to make them more attractive to those they are trying to separate from service.

Golden Handshake programs are many and varied. Your personnel office is the best source of precise details of the program offered educators in your system. Generally, the window of opportunity for taking advantage of early retirement programs is limited; so you must be prepared to accept or reject such offers on short notice.

Basically, early retirement programs give either: (1) the option of full retirement with some adjusted reduction in benefit; or (2) partial retirement with part-time employment for a stipulated number of years to offset reduction of benefits under the standard formula.

The first, or adjusted formula, program permits you to make a clean break from your position. It leaves you free to relocate, to change careers, to do as you wish with the rest of your life. The second, or part-time employment, program generally results in a higher retirement income than you would receive under the adjusted formula. The part-time employment programs leave you tied to your present employer and permit you to remain active in your profession.

Pete P. retired from teaching under a Golden Handshake program which offered early retirement under an adjusted formula. He decided that this was his opportunity to study law. His studies were subsidized in part by his retirement benefit. After he was admitted to practice he worked for a time in the public defender's office. Then he left to set up practice on his own. He was at last doing what he had always wanted to do. His mature years were an advantage rather than a handicap. He had a profession where there was an opportunity for self-employment with no mandatory retirement age. Unlike most attorneys in early years of practice, he had an assured income to tide him over the lean times.

Joan H. always wanted to be an architect. She had become a teacher instead. She, too, retired under an adjusted benefit program. She left the area where she had taught for 25 years and found employment in an architect's office in another state. She was able to accept the modest salary offered because she had her retirement annuity to supplement her take-home pay. She never became an architect, but, for her, she was near enough.

Ed W., on the other hand, retired as a school psychologist under a part-time employment program. He contracted to do testing for the special education program for the number of hours required in his early retirement agreement. The balance of his time was used to establish a family counseling practice. He continued to live in the same town, to associate with old friends and to work in a familiar setting. He was pleased to have the security of assured part-time employment to add to his retirement benefits.

Mark L., using the same type of part-time employment program, contracted to work as a substitute teacher for the stipulated number of hours. He soon wearied of the variety of assignments. He felt his professional skills were not fully utilized. He had no reduction in net income but he wasn't really free to follow his dreams. He bitterly regretted his choice.

Golden handshake programs may be a blessing for employers eager to cut costs, but they aren't the right answer for every educator.

Examine the hazards and the benefits of such programs on a long range basis before you make a decision to choose early retirement.

Career Change

It may be wise to consider "stepping out" of teaching or administration for a time to seek a new career. In most retirement systems your rights are assured after a certain number of years in the system, so you lose only a few "years of service" if you leave the system temporarily. If you are in one of the states such as California where teachers are not eligible for social security, you may find that after 10 years in another career your covered employment will give you substantial additional benefits.

What careers are open to teachers and administrators outside of education? Who wants to hire a 50-year old educator when there are scores of bright young college graduates seeking employment?

One of the new career opportunities lies in the field of computers. The spread of high technology into education, the demand for computer literacy as a prerequisite to graduation, and the almost insatiable need for good educational software combine to make educational software design a thriving business. There are thousands of programmers skilled in the technology of programming who know absolutely nothing about education. They do not know how to design a program that does more than offer drill and practice. They do not know what you know about curriculum development, about simulation, about development of thinking skills. It is far easier to team an educator with a programmer than it is to make an educator out of a programmer. The teaching skills you have spent years learning and practicing are design skills needed in the microcomputer educational software field.

Development in artificial intelligence, interactive video, and information retrieval systems offer other career opportunities for professional educators.

Public service outside of education is another area of

career opportunity for the professional educator. There is need for capable, mature persons to work in federal, state, and local government positions. In most jurisdictions, merit system regulations cover such jobs. You must take and pass civil service examinations with high enough scores to qualify for placement on the list of eligibles. If you are seriously considering a change of career, go to your public library. Ask to see the examination announcements for federal, state, and local government job openings. File applications for every examination for which you are qualified. You may not pass the first few you take, but with practice you will soon find yourself "exam wise." Then you will be ready to take examinations for the jobs you really want. The final step of a civil service examination is usually a "qualification appraisal panel" or an oral examination. That is where you will find your years of teaching, your communication skills, and your self-confidence will pay off. Your poise and maturity will gain you high marks.

There is growing need in private industry for competent, mature individuals to serve in management capacities. Businesses need reliable employees who understand the importance of the work ethic and who know how to work with and develop young employees.

Many former educators have found new careers in real estate, in financial institutions, and in politics. Many are finding new careers in the field of gerontology.

If coping with the problems of adolescents has exhausted your energy and caused your dedication to the development of young minds to flag, perhaps it is time to turn to helping those at the other end of life's continuum—the aged.

The late Dr. Ethel Percy Andrus, founder of the American Association of Retired Persons, was an educator, a dedicated member of the profession. In the words of one of her former students, "She was my principal at Los Angeles' Lincoln High School. I recall her flaming red hair flying behind her as she ran up and down the playing fields cheering her students on. She loved every one of her students but administered her school with strict discipline." She carried that love for the individual and that dedication to helping people to lead a better life into the field of gerontology where she achieved a dramatic success.

Gerontologists provide direct services to older adults in senior centers, nursing homes, hospitals, and other facilities. They teach young people about aging and about older people. Some gerontologists engage in research in the field of aging and in the needs of older persons. Others assist in the development of public policy relating to services for older Americans. Still others act as advocates for the elderly, contacting and educating members of local, state and federal governing bodies. Some, such as Dr. Andrus, perform all of these roles and more.

Americans age 65 or older constitute the most rapidly growing segment of population in the United States. According to material published by the Institute of Lifetime Learning (American Association of Retired Persons) and the Western Gerontological Society:

"These demographic facts raise important questions about the future of the nation's economy, subsequent public policy and public expenditures for social security, health care and social services, levels of taxation, employment opportunities and retirement, continuing education and the quality of life of the older population. By participating in the growing number of programs and services for older Americans you can find answers to these questions.... If you participate in the field of aging, you will find endless opportunities to make new friends among other people who are attracted to this interesting and exciting field."

You can enter the field of gerontology at any age. There are programs to train paraprofessionals at many community colleges. Some colleges and universities offer degrees in gerontology. Check with your local library for a listing of institutions offering such programs. You will find the listing in the AGHE National Directory of Educational Programs in Gerontology.

These are but a few of the opportunities which exist for educators desiring to change careers and to find full-time employment in another field. There are many other opportunities available for those who wish to supplement early retirement benefits with part-time employment.

Part-Time Employment

You will have 50 hours a week to fill with meaningful activity when you retire. Some of those hours can be used to supplement your retirement income. A part-time job, as one retired educator put it, can give you the best of both worlds—you can have a two day work week and a five day weekend.

Where can you find a part-time job? Often you will find employment opportunities in unexpected places. The nearby wine tasting room you passed every day on your way to work may need extra help on weekends or during the summer tourist season. The company which catered your daughter's wedding reception may need someone to serve food or drinks. The department store where you have shopped for years may need your services during heavy shopping periods. Your school district may need vacation relief for clerical staff. Have you listened to employer's complaints about how difficult it is to secure reliable help? Mature persons who understand responsibility are just the employees they are seeking—particularly, reliable persons willing to fill in on short notice, willing to work a few hours per week.

For those who want part-time employment in the field of education, there are openings for substitute teachers, for college evening class instructors, for research assistants, for readers, for teacher's aides, for persons to assist blind or handicapped students. Staff development programs are frequently in the market for qualified trainers. Textbook publishers often hire retired educators as consultants. Writing "how to" articles for teacher's or parent's magazines is a possibility worth exploring. Tutoring college students is an opportunity to teach on a one-to-one basis.

Almost every occupational field provides part-time employment opportunities if you are willing to use your skills and imagination to find openings.

One retired educator found her part-time employment opportunity with a travel agency specializing in tours for senior citizens. She traveled the world as a tour leader.

Another educator, familiar with the need of working parents to find after-school care for their children, set herself up as a "care broker." She found many women willing to provide service for one or two children and placed youngsters with them. She screened the children and the care providers. For a fee she matched child and provider.

Along the same lines, another retired educator acted as a "care broker" for older persons. She found reliable household help; found persons willing to provide transportation to shopping, entertainment, or doctor's appointments; and found men and women who would provide handyman-type services. She checked all prospective employees and required them to be trained and bonded. Once she had reliable help available, she solicited clients through senior centers and newspaper advertisements. She charged her clients a modest fee for assuring them reliable assistance.

The secret of finding part-time employment is the same magic slogan that created fortunes for entrepreneurs around the world — find a need and fill it.

Peace Corps

"Ask not what your country can do for you. Ask what you can do for your country," admonished President John F. Kennedy.

You have developed many skills and abilities during your years of service as an educational professional. You have learned to be self-directed. You have proven intellectual capacity. You have developed an ability to organize work. You know how to stretch scarce resources to cover unmet needs. You have social skills and the ability to work with people of various ages and backgrounds. And above all, you have self-confidence.

Now you are at that awkward age—old enough to take early retirement, yet too young to stop working. There must be some place where they need your skills and abilities, some place where age is an advantage, not a handicap. There must be some place where you can prove that Americans are concerned citizens of the world.

The Peace Corps is that place.

Developing countries all over the world need educational professionals to help enlarge and improve their educational systems. Until they are able to train their own teachers in sufficient numbers, these countries desperately need Peace Corps volunteers for assignment in almost every field of education. They need them in teacher training, secondary and university education, linguistics, math and science, English, speech therapy, educational testing, special education, business, and community development. The list is long because the need is great.

The Peace Corps considers older Americans, particularly retired teachers, to be a vital link in the development chain. The Corps recognizes that no other single group has more to offer in terms of experience, maturity, and demonstrated ability.

You read earlier the story of 71-year old Virginia Spray who found the respect that teachers miss in American classrooms in her work with students in Liberia. Stories similar to Virginia's fill Peace Corps literature.

"Jean Stritter, 60, taught math and science in a remote mountain village high school in Nepal. She had been a math teacher in New England for 10 years prior to joining the Peace Corps. In Nepal, she taught seventh, eighth and ninth graders. She also tried to improve curriculum development and to train teachers in modern techniques. She developed a library for the school and acquired more than 150 illustrated American books and magazines. Jean lived in a one-story house built with bricks and stones and mortared with mud. It had a thatched porch which looked out on the Himalayas. While maintaining that it was difficult to measure accomplishments in teaching, she said her most satisfying experience was the day-to-day contact with her students; and she went away 'with the people deeply rooted in my heart'."

There are teachers serving as Peace Corps volunteers all over the world.

Dennis Drake served as an educator for the deaf in the Philippines.

Alma Lopez served as a speech pathologist and teacher trainer in Asuncion, the capital of Paraguay.

Brian K. Maloney taught basic science and English in the small village of Kolonga in the South Pacific Kingdom of Tonga.

All of these teachers report that they gained as much as they gave. They lived in foreign countries not as outsiders, not as tourists, but as valued parts of the local society. No amount of foreign travel could have contributed as much to their understanding of the strengths and problems of developing countries.

The Peace Corps pays volunteers a monthly living allowance which covers basic housing, food, and incidental expenses while in the field. When they return home they typically receive $4,200 for a two-year assignment. They receive language, technical and cross cultural training to help them to adjust and perform duties in the assigned country.

Married couples are eligible and encouraged to serve if both can work and wish to be volunteers. And best of all, there is no age limit.

Miss Lillian, President Carter's mother, served in the Peace Corps when she was in her 70s.

Odi Long, 81, has served longer than any other Peace Corps volunteer. He joined the service in 1967, the same day he retired after 41 years with AT&T in Illinois.

If you are looking for a way to cap your years of service with a magnificent new career, the Peace Corps recruiters guarantee that you find that opportunity with them.

10 *What Do You Do After You Get The Gold Watch?*

Y ou have finally reached the end of your countdown to retirement. Departure day has come and gone. The parties are over. You are free. You are responsible to no one. You are responsible for nothing. Suddenly your life has no structure. There is no duty to compel you to do anything other than that which you wish to do.

You are like a person who has just won a million dollars. You are gainfully unemployed. What are you going to do with the next 30 years of your life?

The Day After 'D Day'

Like most retirees, you will go through a decompression period. You will act as if you were on a summer holiday. You may travel. Many retirees do. You may work around the house. You may catch up on long delayed chores. Many retirees do. You may play golf or tennis. You may read a novel or two. Many retirees do.

128

You may stay up late at night and sleep late in the morning. You may revel in the delight of inactivity. That, too, is a normal and natural reaction to relief from pressure. When the first hint of autumn arrives you will think about going back to work. Many retirees do. You will find old habits hard to break. That is the time when you realize there is no job. That is the time when you realize that you need a plan.

You want your retirement to be a rich reward for years of dedication to the needs of others. You do not want your life to be an endless succession of empty, wasted days from here to eternity.

This chapter and those which follow will assist you in planning your post-retirement activity. With a plan you can greet the days after "D day" with excitement rather than dread. Now is the time to go back to Chapter 2. Reread the section concerning goals. Think again about your personality. Imagine yourself in various roles. What really gives you pleasure? What makes you uncomfortable?

After you make your self-analysis you can better evaluate the suggestions for post-retirement activity which follow. Perhaps none will appeal to you. In that case you should spend some time talking with retired persons whom you admire. Ask them what keeps them full of enthusiasm for life. Ask them how they fill their free time. You may find in their experience answers to your question, "What do I do now?"

Some retired educators feel that it is wrong to have scheduled activities which keep them busy day after day. They dream of the time when they will be free to do nothing. That dream can turn into a nightmare in a very short time.

Togetherness
Part of the nightmare comes from a new kind of

stress—the stress of adjustment to a new lifestyle. One of the primary causes of discord in the lives of many retired couples is the inability to adjust to the amount of time they now have together. All the years of their married life they had time away from each other. Each had his or her own job. Each had individual interests. Now there are no jobs to take them away from each other into separate worlds. Both men and women have difficulty adjusting to the new pattern of life. Those difficulties breed bitterness and resentment. Without a realistic appraisal of the cause of the conflict, small annoyances frequently grow into irreconcilable differences and divorce.

Howard and Elizabeth M. retired from their teaching positions the same day. They celebrated their retirement and their 35th wedding anniversary simultaneously. There was no cloud to mar the future. Happily married, free from financial and child-rearing worries, they saw nothing but happiness ahead.

They had no plans for activities to fill their days. Howard was at home all day with too little to do. At first he noticed how Elizabeth managed the household chores. Then he tried to persuade her to become better organized. The second week he became critical of the meals she prepared. By the third week of retirement Elizabeth, frustrated and angry, suggested that Howard could either get a job or a divorce. Sensible people that they were, they recognized the cause of the problem. That day they developed schedules which gave them time to be away from each other, time to pursue independent interests.

Other couples faced with the same problem, resolved it by divorce. That solution may reflect more than the stress of retirement. It may simply be the culmination of long-suppressed unhappiness with each other. Divorce can be as liberating as retirement in such cases. On the other hand, examination of aspects of the problems which lie below the surface can bring husband and wife to an understanding of each other's needs.

Women do not retire. They leave their positions in the world of work just as men do. Nevertheless, they must continue the daily routine of household chores. Three meals a day become an endless cycle of meal planning, cooking and dish washing. Work expands to fit the time available until life is a continuous round of dull, repetitive tasks. The working woman risks frustration and irritation if she has not planned activities to take her away from household tasks after retirement. Her role as a professional has vanished. Boring tasks replace those with some ego satisfying activity.

This gloomy picture of unfulfilled life is not exaggerated. Just as stress in the workplace is real, so, too, is stress in retirement. The fortunate aspect of stress in retirement is that it is easily alleviated. Solution of the problem lies in awareness of the hazards which arise from days filled with dull, pointless pursuits.

You do not have to fall into the trap of inactivity. Nor do you have to be busy at tasks you dislike. You do not have to commit suicide on the installment plan. Nor do you have to substitute the strait jacket of planned activity for the constraint of the position you just left. You don't have to ruin your marriage. You have many options open to you.

A recent survey of retired educators asked the question, "What is important to you?" The answers ranked by frequency of response were:
- Continuing education
- Daytime cultural events
- Contemplative reading
- More time for socializing
- More time for family

- Continuation of old hobbies
- Development of new hobbies
- Sports
- Travel

Women ranked high on their lists the need for counseling about second career opportunities. Both men and women felt that peer counseling was important to successful retirement.

Choose the life you want. Don't let your mind decay through lack of use.

Continuing Education

Retirement provides a stress-free time to expand your knowledge. You are no longer under pressure to publish or perish. You are free to explore any subject which intrigues you. You can take courses in any subject, free of worry about grades or failure. You will find that your mind suddenly becomes more creative. Your enthusiasm for learning will be as great as it was on your first day of school. You will find there is a productive linkage between play and learning.

Travel And Learn

The American Institute for Foreign Study, an international educational travel organization, offers more than 100 itineraries of various lengths. Programs are open to adults as well as younger students. The organization offers up to $800 in scholarship assistance to those who have participated as host families in the AIFS Cultural Exchange.

Learning Holidays Abroad are specifically for adults. The holidays give the traveler an opportunity to discover art, history, music, politics, and everyday living in Europe and Mexico. For information and an application, contact the American Institute for Foreign Study, 102 Greenwich Ave., Greenwich, CT 06830.

Elderhostel combines the best traditions of education and hosteling, specifically for older citizens who want to reach out for new experiences.

Elderhostel is a network of over 800 colleges, universities, independent schools, folk schools and other educational institutions in the U.S., Canada and Europe. These institutions offer special, low cost, short term, residential, academic programs for older adults. The Elderhostel experience provides an informal atmosphere where the individual is important.

Your accommodations are in dormitories and other residential facilities near classrooms and dining halls. You eat meals in regular college cafeterias with other students.

Elderhostel promises that every program will be different—from the courses to the accommodations.

There is no course credit. There are no examinations, no grades, and no required homework.

The program charge is an all inclusive fee. In a typical program the fee includes:
- Registration
- Six nights accommodations
- All meals—Sunday evening through Saturday breakfast
- Five days of classes
- All courses listed in the program
- A variety of extracurricular activities.

How much is the charge? Prepare for good news. The maximum charge per person per week in the continental United States is $225. The charge is $245 in Canada. In Alaska the charge is $260. Hawaiian programs cost $230. Overseas programs run two to three weeks. The charge for these programs cover almost all expenses. They include round trip airfare. They also include all within-the-country travel, full room and board, tuition at the universities, admission fees to historical sites, and local excursions. Overseas program costs range from approximately $1,470 to $3,842. The cost depends upon the country.

Courses in the United States are many and varied. You can take a course in personal finance at Eastern Maine Tech in Bangor, Maine. You can study the Revolutionary War in the Lower Hudson at St. Thomas Aquinas College in Southeastern Rockland County, New York. You can get acquainted with computers at Western Illinois University in Macomb, Illinois. You can study the writings of John Steinbeck at San Francisco State University, San Francisco, California. You can spend a week at the Yosemite Institute, Yosemite National Park, California, studying the human and natural history of the park.

You can study the Middle East/Arab-Israeli conflict at Haifa University, Israel. You can study cows, cheese, chocolates and mountains in Switzerland. You can experience international living in France, Germany, India, or Mexico. All of these opportunities were available during a recent summer. Check the latest catalog for current courses. The Elderhostel catalog is available from:

Elderhostel
80 Boylston Street, Suite 400,
Boston, MA 02116.

Are you interested in archeology? Each summer and fall many archeological activities occur in the United States, Canada, and Mexico. They provide visitors a special view of the past. Some of the projects offer opportunities for volunteers to participate in the work. *Archeology* magazine publishes an annual travel guide which lists project sites and directions for reaching them. The listings give thumbnail sketches of the historical significance of each site. They also state whether volunteers are welcome, how long they must agree to participate and the extent of experience required. Many of the projects do accept volunteers. Some ask that you have some previous field work experience. Others will take willing but untrained persons. Still others require that untrained volunteers take a field school course at a designated college or university. If you have always wanted to uncover history, one of the projects listed will give you that chance.

The Smithsonian Institution offers both domestic and foreign study tours under the guidance of museum curators or visiting scholars. Whether it is to be whale watching in Baja California, a trip down the Mississippi on a steamboat, or a sailing adventure from the Canary Islands to Martinique, the Smithsonian will teach you while you are having fun.

If you prefer to limit your learning experiences to Washington, D.C., the Smithsonian offers seminars on topics ranging from anthropology to space exploration. You can obtain information on Smithsonian study tours and seminars by writing to:

National Associates
Capital Gallery 455
Smithsonian Institution
Washington, D.C. 20560.

You may call 202/287-3362 for study tour brochures. For seminar brochures call 202/357-1350.

The Smithsonian programs are open only to Smithsonian Associates. To become a member you need only pay a modest membership fee. Write to Smithsonian Associates, 900 Jefferson Drive, Washington, D.C. 20560, for information about membership.

The American Museum of Natural History, New York, N.Y., also offers a wide variety of study tours under the direction of museum curators or scholars in the particular field.

For more information on what is available in your community, contact your local gallery or museum.

Universities and colleges also offer extensive opportunities to travel and learn. You will find a program which fits your specific interest if you explore the possibilities.

Learn At Home

You do not have to leave home to continue to be a learner. You can take courses through university extension programs, adult education classes, or community college programs.

Many public and private universities throughout the United States offer home study courses through their extension programs. Some extension programs also offer classes in locations away from the university. As you probably already know, extension program courses require homework and examinations. They rarely permit application of the credits earned to fulfillment of requirements for degrees.

If you live near a university so that you are able to attend regular classes, you can, of course, earn advanced degrees by enrolling as a regular student. Some retired educators eager to explore new careers do just that. They find that learning a new subject stimulates their mental capacities and keeps them young.

A typical program for retired persons called EGO is sponsored by California State University, San Diego. EGO is the acronym for Educational Growth Opportunities. The program offers classes of six to eight weeks duration without credit or examination. Volunteers, retired university professors, regular professors, and lay people knowledgeable in the particular field teach the classes. Course offerings range from study of foreign languages to marine biology. There are courses in music, art, literature, science, and math. Demand governs class offerings. Students join the EGO program by paying a small fee and then pay course fees of various amounts. Membership carries with it some of the same privileges offered regular students of the university.

If you have an interest in the operation of the EGO program, you may write to:

EGO
4075 Park Blvd.,
San Diego, CA 92103.

You do not have to attend classes to continue learning. In every city library there are extensive collections of fiction and nonfiction, biography and autobiography. Through inter-library loans you can supplement the materials available in your local library. If you want to become an expert in some field, the library is the place to start. Some libraries now provide computer access to extensive databases. These provide research capability formerly available only to persons with access to great university libraries or the Library of Congress. When it comes to information the key to retrieval is time. As a retired person, you have that key.

Libraries will provide you with the printed word. If you want to learn what the experts are saying in person, you need to check your Sunday papers for notices of lectures being given by learned scholars, politicians, business leaders, writers, and experts in various other fields. You could spend your life going to lectures if you attended all that are available.

Cultural Events

Many retired educators prefer to attend the theater, concerts, lectures, and other events in the daytime rather than in the evening. The reasons for this preference are valid. Fear of crime is one fear that retired persons give for reluctance to go out at night. That fear is a legitimate one. Inadequate public transportation in the evening is another reason for reluctance to attend evening performances. That, too, is a legitimate complaint. Higher costs of evening performances is also cited as a reason for not attending. That is also a valid argument.

Matinee performances are unfortunately often limited to one or two a week. This often results in scheduling conflicts. You sometimes must choose between seeing a play or hearing a concert. You must remember not to schedule other activities on those afternoons when you have tickets for the ballet.

That is the bad news. The good news is that daytime, midweek cultural events are usually less expensive to attend. It is easier to secure tickets. There is a higher probability that you can obtain senior citizen rates. Best of all, you can use public transportation to reach the theater or concert hall. This avoids the expense and difficulty of parking your car.

Because you live in a community distant from a city where there is a symphony orchestra, ballet, or opera company, you need not forego enjoyment of cultural events.

Margaret P. escaped from her duties as a third grade teacher into the world of music. Her favorite form of music was opera. When she retired she organized a group of fellow opera lovers in her small town. They bought season tickets to the opera in the major metropolitan center nearest them. The group studied each opera before they attended the performance. They listened to recordings made by various performers singing the roles they were about to hear. On the day of the performance, they chartered a mini-van to travel to the city. Margaret and her friends stretched their minds and their spirits. They did not permit distance or age keep them from the recreation they most enjoyed.

You don't need to be an opera buff to do what Margaret and her friends did. There are many other mind-stretching activities available during daytime hours. Many communities schedule forum or town hall type meetings around noontime. Some cities have Arm Chair Cruise performances scheduled in the afternoon.

If you have an interest in art, you will find more galleries open during the day than in the evening.

Nature and science museums are open during day-time hours. They are less crowded midweek than on weekends. Exhibits and historic sites are more frequently open during the day than during evening hours. They, too, are less crowded on weekdays than they are on Saturdays and Sundays.

If you live some distance from a city where there are museums, galleries, public forums, and similar events, you can do as Margaret did. Public transportation companies frequently have vans available for small group charter. If you can afford the luxury and your group is small consider the cost of hiring a limousine as a means of transportation which relieves you of either the constraints of public transportation schedules or the discomfort of driving yourself.

Summary

The key to a successful career as a retired person is identical to the key to a successful career as an educator. Know what you want to do, prepare to do it, and implement your plan.

Don't go to bed at night without something to accomplish when you rise the next morning. Plan to accomplish at least one objective each day.

Keep your mind stimulated by learning something new or by expanding your insight into a familiar field. Combine play with learning. Challenge conventional wisdom which holds that if there is no pain there is no gain. The informed mind at play is responsible for the major innovations in the sciences: natural, social and political.

You don't have to spend all of your time on cultural activities or lifelong learning experiences to fill your days with activity.

You can share some of your free time helping others.

11 | *Retire To Community Service*

Every day, in every city and town in the United States, there are jobs waiting for people who are willing to work without pay. Many organizations could not exist if it were not for unpaid, volunteer assistance. Volunteers do everything from answering phones to searching for lost airplanes.

For those who volunteer the rewards are substantial. Some find it a cure for loneliness. Others find it a way to feel needed and important. Almost all volunteers find that their activities fill a basic need to accomplish something each day. That sense of achievement makes the difference between living and existing.

Federally Sponsored Volunteer Programs

Volunteer programs such as Foster Grandparents and the Senior Companion Programs sponsored by the federal government are open only to individuals over 60 with low incomes. These programs provide modest tax-free stipends, transportation allowances, hot meals while on duty and an annual physical examination. Because you have used your countdown to retirement wisely, you will probably have too much income to qualify for either of these volunteer programs. On the other hand, for those with retirement incomes eroded by inflation, these are welcome opportunities to help others while being helped financially themselves.

Foster Grandparents provide companionship and guidance for emotionally, physically, and mentally handicapped children. Abused, or neglected children or those involved in the juvenile justice system are also the concern of Foster Grandparents.

Jenny has been a Foster Grandparent for 11 years. She works with kindergarten children during the school year. She helps those children who need a little extra attention and love. In the summer, just to keep busy, Jenny works with the girls in juvenile hall. Jenny taught for 20 years before she retired. She acquired virtually no teacher retirement system benefits because her husband's employment as a steel worker took them from state to state. She was barely able to support herself on her social security survivor's benefits after her husband died.

The Senior Companion program provides assistance to adults with physical or mental impairments. The Senior Companions help homebound elderly persons continue independent living. The Companions also serve in institutions where they work with patients about to go home. They serve not only as companions but act as advocates. They link their clients to appropriate community services. They intercede to correct utility bill disputes and to assist in settlement of other consumer complaints.

Ada S. is a Senior Companion. She, too, is a retired educator with less than adequate retirement benefits.

Ada supplements her retirement income with the stipend from the Senior Companion program. She goes daily to help a widow who is blind and crippled by arthritis. With Ada's help, her client is able to stay out of an institution. With her Senior Companion stipend, Ada is also able to live independently.

The Retired Senior Volunteer Program (RSVP), also sponsored by the federal government, has no income requirements. Those who wish to become RSVP volunteers must be at least 60 years old and retired. RSVP volunteers serve in senior citizen centers, in senior citizen craft cooperatives, in hospitals, nursing homes, schools and crisis centers. They assist in projects dealing with health care delivery, nutrition, skyrocketing utility rates and fixed income counseling. Volunteers choose assignments from a broad list of possibilities compiled by the local RSVP office. Other than assistance with transportation, volunteers receive no compensation for their work. Their reward comes from giving. As one volunteer said, "giving of yourself as a volunteer is a way to gain life."

Museums Need You

You have helped to support at least one museum or art gallery over the years through your membership dues and contributions. Welcome as that support is, it is not enough. Few museums are so generously endowed that they are able to hire all the help that a well-run institution requires. Most museums depend heavily upon the assistance of volunteers to supplement endowments and private contributions.

Museum volunteers work behind the scenes to keep the institutions operating smoothly. Volunteers assist in cataloging collections. They help to install exhibits, prepare labels, and organize materials. They assist in fund raising activities through membership guilds.

The part of volunteer museum service that many enjoy most is the opportunity to become docents. Docent means an unpaid teacher. What could be a better job for a retired educator? Docents are trained to be knowledgeable about the museum's holdings through the classes that sometimes run as long as two years. Once trained the docent conducts tours through the museum and explains the exhibits.

In some smaller museums volunteers actually staff the building during public visiting hours. They act as clerks in the gift shop, as security guards, and as tour guides. When the museum day is over they assist with the custodial chores and arrange new exhibits. In their spare time they raise funds to support the enterprise.

Whatever the size of your community, there is probably a local history museum or art gallery which would welcome your help.

Social Service

Whether it is a suicide prevention hotline, a sanctuary for battered women, an emergency facility for abused or neglected children, a dining room for the hungry, or a shelter for the homeless, chances are that service would not exist were it not for volunteers.

Hospitals, public and private, rely upon volunteers to provide non-medical assistance to patients and their families.

As the government cut back funding for assistance to the less fortunate, the need for volunteer assistance increased. There are more problems, more crises, more needs than limited public and private resources can meet.

If you speak a foreign language, you can help as a translator. You can comfort a child if you have a warm and loving heart. You can help feed the needy if you can cook or serve meals. You can answer hotline phones, becoming a lifeline for a seriously troubled person, if you have free time.

Educators know how much troubled youth and their families need friends. Those friends can cut through bureaucratic red tape. They can explain what assistance is available and how to secure it. They can help to prevent juvenile delinquency. They can keep students from slipping through the gaps in the so-called safety net.

The volunteers who run hospital gift shops, who man the book and magazine delivery carts, who stop to chat with a frightened patient, humanize the atmosphere of hospitals. When major illnesses strike, patients and their families need more support than busy doctors and overworked nurses can give. Volunteers fill that need.

If social service appeals to you, there are endless opportunities for you to serve. You have only to volunteer.

There are other ways to serve your community which might not occur to you.

Jury Duty

Have you ever watched the legal system in action? Have you seen the real life drama that occurs daily in our courtrooms? If you would like to be a part—an integral part—of our system of justice, you can, in many jurisdictions, ask that your name be put on the list of prospective jurors. Many retired people with good hearing and eyesight have added to the strength of our legal system by serving on either trial juries or investigative grand juries.

The trial jury selection process relies on the judgment of the defense and prosecution attorneys as to juror qualification. The court may call you frequently as a potential juror. Nevertheless, you may serve only if you survive the hazards of questioning and preemptory challenges. For those interested in the law, simply watching the process of determining guilt or innocence can be a fascinating hobby.

Grand jurors are nominated by the judges of the court and, after selection, serve for a stipulated period of time. Grand juries serve two main functions. First, they have responsibility for determining if an accused person should be tried. They look at the evidence and, if in their judgment it is substantial, they bring indictments against persons suspected of criminal acts. The second function of the grand jury is to look into the conduct of public officials, the expenditure of public funds, and the functioning of local government. It is in this second capacity that those interested in the effective functioning of government find the most satisfaction. If you have interest in serving on a grand jury, investigate the nominating process and make an effort to have your name submitted.

Teacher's Aide

Not all teacher's aides are paid for their services. In some schools administrators welcome the assistance of volunteers to help teachers with playground supervision before school, at recess and lunch times. In other schools where large class sizes are fiscally unavoidable, unpaid volunteers who are qualified teachers act as volunteer teacher's aides. These unpaid aides do not supplant but supplement the work of paid aides. They assure that children who need extra attention receive that assistance promptly before they fall behind their classmates. Some volunteers are used to provide special classes in art, music and other extracurricular activities. In every school there are unmet needs caused by declining resources and amplified demands for curricular offerings. The push for excellence, for more math and science classes, for more emphasis of writing and thinking skills, leave most teachers frantic to find time to do all of the things that must be done. You as an educator know what it feels like to try to do the work of two with only one head and one pair of hands. Offering your services as a part-time volunteer teacher's aide is one way that you can reach out a hand to an overworked colleague.

Tutor

As an educator you know better than anyone how frequently students need more attention than they can obtain from the teacher or the teacher's aide. Students who drop behind their classmates in the early years go on to become the troubled teens who disturb the higher grades. Whether children or adolescents, these students need the help of tutors who can work with them on a one-to-one basis. There are many programs supported by special grants or project funds designed to provide such special tutors for hard-to-teach youngsters. All too frequently these programs falter because there are not enough volunteer tutors available to staff the projects. If you have an interest in the challenge of rescuing the youngsters who are potential dropouts or juvenile delinquents, contact your local school district. Ask if they have a volunteer tutor program. Let them know that you are available. If there is not a formal program in operation, contact the teacher organization or PTA and let them know that you are willing to tutor youngsters who need extra help. A few hours of your time may mean a productive rather than a dependent life for a troubled child. You can make the difference.

Boards And Commissions

We are surrounded by governmental agencies. They are under the supervision of elected officials. Civil servants, hired through a merit selection process, staff the offices. However, in addition to elected officials and civil servants, there are hundreds of appointed boards and commissions in every city and state which regulate our lives and which are part of the public policy making process.

Would you like to have your voice heard in the decision making process? You can become an appointed member of the local planning commission, the mental health advisory board, the consumers council, the water quality control board, the council on aging, or any of the dozens of other boards and commissions which flourish in your area.

Examine your particular interests and qualifications. Put together a convincing resume of your experience and qualifications. Become a board or commission watcher. Attend each meeting and listen carefully to discussion of agenda items. Become as knowledgeable about the affairs of the organization as you can as an outsider. When you are thoroughly familiar with the work of the group, it is time to study the politics of appointment. Who appoints? Who recommends individuals for appointment? On what bases are appointments made? Are they political payoffs? Are they based on selection of persons outstanding in a certain field? Do those responsible for appointments look for representatives of particular interest groups? Must you be a friend or a supporter of an elected official?

By the time you have researched the qualifications, the work of the board and the politics of appointment, you will be ready to make your application. You will have your support group ready to advance your candidacy. You will be more than ready to serve if appointed. Don't be dismayed if appointment eludes you the first time you apply. Determine, if you can, the reason that you were not considered. Perhaps you are not as qualified as you thought. Perhaps another board or commission would be a better choice. If you have a determination to serve, you will develop the skills and connections needed.

If you would like to have more information on serving on boards and commissions, write to the Consumers Affairs Program Department, American Association of Retired Persons, 1909 K street N.W., Washington, D.C. 20049. Ask for their booklet, "How To Get Appointed To A Board Or Commission: A Guide For Older Citizens."

Organizations

Are you a joiner? Would you like to be part of an organization which has a purpose?

If you want to continue to be part of life after you retire, there are many organizations which offer opportunities to enjoy the company of like-minded individuals while contributing to the well-being of your fellow man or woman.

The American Association of Retired Persons and its affiliated organization, the National Retired Teachers Association, offer members many activities and services. [See Chapter 8.]

League Of Women Voters

If you have an interest in knowing the pros and cons of most matters of public policy, the League of Women Voters is the organization for you to join. The League is both a study and an action organization. Because of its emphasis on in-depth study of issues relating to public policy, League members become very knowledgeable about the operation of government. Assigned members watch and report on the conduct of the public business. Leagues sponsor candidates' nights to permit every candidate a public forum.

Because the League of Women Voters has built a solid reputation for non-partisanship, members of all political parties find the organization a source of unbiased information. Active League members never go to bed at night wondering what they will do to keep busy tomorrow. There is always an issue to study, there is always research to do, and there is always action to take.

In the interest of full sexual equality, League membership is open to men as well as women. The League also encourages its members to work for the political parties and candidates of their choice, though not as League members but simply as concerned citizens.

Political Parties And Pressure Groups

Educators are well aware of the influence of politics on education. Many are equally aware of the influence of educators on politics. A survey of elected officials reveals that large numbers of educators are among holders of public office.

Both major political parties welcome persons willing to contribute time and/or money to campaigns. At the national level money is more welcome than manpower. At local campaign levels those needs are more evenly balanced. You will find it easier to break into active party politics by volunteering to work for local office candidates than by trying to work for a presidential or U.S. senatorial candidate. If you are a novice in political campaign work, you must expect to work at less glamorous chores at first. Don't let walking precincts or stuffing envelopes continue to be the sum of your activity. Become part of the decision making process if you want your voice heard.

Do your homework before you become involved. What is the political party governance structure in your state? Do you have a ward committee or a county central committee? Are the members elected or appointed? How does the party select delegates to caucuses or party conventions? Who controls the party in your area? Answers to these questions will help you identify opportunities open to you.

Contact your congressman and U.S. senator if you have an interest in national politics. Visit their local offices to become acquainted with their field staff. Volunteer to contribute money and to assist in their next campaign if you support their candidacies. Once they have your name they will invite you to fund raisers. Prepare to pay for some very costly meals. One hundred dollar-a-plate luncheons and $500 a plate dinners are not uncommon. The iron law of politics is simple. The larger your contribution, the more valued your influence. This may sound cynical, but it is true in this time of very costly campaigns.

Contact your state and local elected officials if you want to be part of less costly political activity. At the local level your effort on behalf of a candidate is more evident and more appreciated. Focus your attention and money on one candidate at a time. You will find that your effort will assist you when you wish to speak to your elected official about the issues of concern to you.

Many retired persons derive great satisfaction from participation in various special interest pressure groups. The Gray Panthers organization is an active protagonist for the interests of older Americans. The Gray Panthers study issues affecting senior citizens in depth. When they have the facts they act. Representatives of the organization often testify before federal and state legislative committees because they can provide factual data about pending legislation. The Gray Panthers and similar consumer and environmental advocacy groups represent the interests of older Americans before boards and commissions with rule making or advisory powers.

Some states have Senior Legislatures. These shadow legislative bodies operate in the same manner as the regular legislative body. Senior citizens in the various legislative districts choose the members of the Senior Legislature. The Senior Legislature considers matters of concern to older Americans. When they reach agreement on proposed legislation they find members of the regular state legislature to author and introduce those measures into the formal legislative process. Members of the Senior Legislature then form an advocacy group to lobby for passage of bills they favor.

Most members of the Senior Legislature are persons who are active in their Senior Citizen Centers.

There are other special interest groups which also support the interests of retired educators.

The American Association of Retired Persons (AARP) and its affiliate, the National Retired Teachers Association (NRTA), are active in both state and federal governmental affairs. The AARP and NRTA represent the interests of retired persons in the areas of consumer protection, employment, health care, and protection of pension benefits. Both organizations have local chapters in cities and towns throughout the United States of America.

The American Federation of Teachers (AFT) and the National Education Association (NEA) both maintain vigorous legislative advocacy programs on behalf of educators and education. You can be part of that effort through continued membership and active participation in either organization after you retire.

You may have other special interests which you wish to support after you retire. If you are at loss for way to make contact with a group representing your particular interest from agriculture to zoology, try the Washington D.C. telephone directory. You will find a copy in your local public library. The directory has two parts: residential and organizational. The organizational directory contains the names, addresses, and phone numbers of organizations which maintain offices in the nation's capital. Those listing represent a full spectrum of special interests and causes.

Write or telephone the organization which represents your particular concern. Ask to be put on the mailing list for information concerning legislation pending before congress which the organization is supporting or opposing.

Once you have that information you can be an independent political activist. Write to your United States senator and to your congressman. Tell them how you feel they should vote on a particular measure. Cite personal reasons why you feel as you do.

If you want to be more knowledgeable about what the government is already doing in that area, there is a book which claims to be the ultimate guide to the largest source of information on earth. The book, written by Matthew Lesko, is *Information U.S.A.*. It is a comprehensive compendium of information about sources of information within the federal bureaucracy. *Information U.S.A.* is available at most book stores.

Churches

John A., a retired high school counselor, knew precisely what he wanted to do when he retired. Within a week of retirement, he volunteered as a missionary for work with the Native Americans in New Mexico.

Ray W., also a retired educator, established an outreach program for his church among the homeless people of his community.

Peter M. went from education into the lay ministry of his church.

153

Esther B. retired from public school administration and into administration of her church's Sunday School program.

All of these retired educators had planned what they wanted to do when they retired. All had been active church members during their working years and they recognized needs that they could fill. Your church is part of your community. You, too, remain part of your community when you take an active part in church affairs.

Summary

Maintain your involvement with life. Don't be a dropout. You have retired to freedom not to boredom. Volunteer work is but one kind of activity for the retired person. It has its advantages and its disadvantages. It provides ego satisfaction. It makes you feel needed. It opens door to new worlds. Those are the advantages.

Too often older volunteers are exploited by those in charge of hospitals, museums, churches, political campaigns or service organizations. Organizations give volunteers menial jobs. The volunteers become an unpaid labor force. Don't permit that to happen to you. Don't let those disadvantages drive you from involvement. Volunteer only for work you want to do. You are a person of value. Make certain that those you volunteer to assist value your contribution. They need you as much or more than you need their work.

There are other ego satisfying activities which you can engage in to fill your free time. We will discuss some of those activities in the next chapter.

12 *Share Your Knowledge*

Along with the peace of mind that comes with planning your retirement well, you have earned another benefit—perhaps the most rewarding of all. For the first time you have options as to how you want to spend your time. As we have pointed out in the previous chapter, there are numerous opportunities to volunteer your services and assist in worthy causes of your choice.

But you also have the option of sharing your knowledge for pay. Over the years you have gained valuable experience which you may wish to market. But remember, sound preparation along with the prior contacts you have made are necessary to ease the transition to your new work and allow you to move according to your schedule. If you have planned well and your retirement income is assured, you have been relieved of the pressure to work in order to survive.

True, part-time work can be a good means of supplementing your retirement income (as we pointed out in Chapter 5), but you now have the option of being gainfully employed to the extent you choose because you want to, not because you have to.

It is important to keep this in mind as you explore the type of work you may wish to do. There is no need to commit yourself to tasks which may prove to be boring or otherwise distasteful. Choose an activity that interests you and that you will find enjoyable and rewarding. Don't forget the old adage, "work ceases to be work if you love it!"

The list of ventures you may wish to undertake is almost inexhaustible. But, it might be useful here to highlight a few examples of "for pay" activities you may wish to explore. Among the most obvious and perhaps easiest to obtain positions are those that are school-connected, such as substitute teaching, tutoring or serving as a teacher's aide. However, such occupations as consulting, writing, multi-level marketing and real estate sales should not be overlooked. Your long experience as a professional educator enhances your opportunities for success in these fields assuming there is interest on your part.

If you have been engaged in part-time work on weekends or during the summer months already, you, of course, may opt to maintain or expand this activity. On the other hand, you might prefer to take the self-employment route as we pointed out in Chapter 5.

Consulting
One would be hard put to find a better way to more directly share your knowledge about education than consulting. Not only are you well positioned to provide your services to schools, county and state offices of education, but there are vast opportunities to be of assistance to private sector companies which target

schools for the sale of their products. In Chapter 5 we stressed the importance of making a list of the skills you have to offer to a prospective employer in the event you were planning to seek part-time employment. Such an exercise is equally important if you plan to do consultant work. When you have made a decision on what you can and would like to do, you must get the word out in appropriate circles.

It is important to develop carefully a strategy to market your services. You might arrange an appointment to solicit the advice of a successful and well-established consultant who provides services in a related field. Or you may attend one of a number of workshops that provide information for persons planning to venture into consulting or the establishment of a small business enterprise.

Most likely you already know the consultative needs of schools in your district. You should talk to principals and supervisors and let them know that when you complete your countdown to retirement you are willing and anxious to provide assistance and advice on some of the pressing problems they face—the ones which your ideas will contribute toward solutions.

County offices of education frequently seek the counsel of experienced teachers before developing, revising or implementing a program that will have an impact on schools within their jurisdictions. State departments of education also welcome teacher input when reviewing their policies and procedures.

Emma W., who retired as an elementary teacher from a school in a large district, agreed to work up to 80 hours per semester in a program designed to assist in orienting new teachers to their jobs. She has found the work enjoyable and rewarding.

Doris W., who retired as a school principal, advises and assists supervisors of student teachers at a local private college. She also teaches a class in school supervision one hour per week. She, too, finds her work enjoyable and rewarding.

Maria N. took early retirement from her position as assistant district superintendent. She now is firmly established as a consultant and provides a wide range of services, including evaluating federally funded programs and organizing and directing a vocational advisory committee of Hispanic women for the state department of education. She also writes proposals for grants for local school districts and does trouble-shooting for county education offices. With the freedom to organize her schedule she finds time for travel and leisure activities.

A stroll through the exhibition hall of any state or national education convention will provide convincing evidence of the vast array of private vendors who are targeting the education market. Everything from books to buses are displayed—computer systems, work books, testing materials, playground equipment and classroom furniture all are in evidence. Most of the displays are supervised by former educators and it requires little imagination to see consultative opportunities emanating from almost every booth.

A couple of examples will suffice. Textbook publishers constantly seek the advice of teachers before and during the development of their materials. Whatever your field of specialization, some publisher is likely to be willing to pay you a consultative fee for your advice if you can demonstrate that you are available and can make a meaningful contribution to their program.

Computer companies that are engaged in providing systems for computer-assisted teaching are also on the lookout for teacher-consultants who can assist them in marketing their products. In addition, developers of education software frequently hire teams of educators to react to products they have under development.

Writing

Remember there is a difference between "wanting to write," "intending to write" and "*writing*." If you have published already, you are a leg up and are off to a head start. If not, you must get started right away. There are any number of writer's magazines on the market. They are filled with ideas. Check your public library or buy copies of books or periodicals and learn everything you can about getting articles published. There are magazines for parents, teachers, journals published by professional teacher organizations as well as commercial magazines which occasionally carry education-oriented articles. Newspapers frequently accept articles for op-ed pages. If you prefer, you may wish to get started on that book you have hoped to write one day.

Another way of getting prepared is to take a writing course. These are almost always available at a nearby community college or through an extension course at a four-year college or university. If you have not discovered it already, good writing is really "re-writing" and the only way to learn to write is to write.

Multi-Level Marketing

Multi-level marketing is used primarily by business firms that want to educate large numbers of consumers about the benefits of their products. After all, happy customers are the best form of advertisement.

The process is to develop a network of sellers called sales associates or consultants, or some such, to function as independent contractors to promote the product through a sales organization they have personally developed. Networking plans are developed and implemented. Among the more widely known firms which use this approach are Amway, Mary Kay and

Tupperware. There are others you may wish to contact.

Although firms that specialize in multi-level marketing techniques vary in their operating procedures, their general approach and goals are similar. A new salesperson, after becoming familiar with the company's products, receives training in a particular method of making sales to consumers. In addition to receiving a percentage of the price their customers pay for products—which may range from 25 to 30 percent, depending upon the company—they are also compensated for recruiting and training other salespersons and frequently receive a percent of the income from their recruits' sales.

Elaine G. and four neighbors were invited to a "skin care class" at the home of a friend. The class was conducted by a Mary Kay "beauty consultant." Elaine was pleased with the complimentary facial she received and purchased some Mary Kay cosmetics. She became intrigued with the Mary Kay marketing technique and after a few weeks decided to become a part-time beauty consultant herself. She was encouraged and assisted by a representative of the company and has attended training and motivational meetings under the supervision of a Mary Kay sales director.

Although Elaine now serves as a beauty consultant only in her spare time, her list of customers is growing. She was able to get started with an investment of less then $100 which she used to purchase a "beauty showcase." She buys her products wholesale from the company and retails them to her customers. She was amazed to discover how easily her teaching skills were transferable to conducting skin care classes and doing motivational work. She is looking forward to taking early retirement next year and plans to devote more time to marketing Mary Kay products. She has even thought of becoming a sales director. If she does and is successful, she expects that her commissions plus retirement income will exceed her present salary as a teacher.

Real Estate

A number of retired teachers are sharing their knowledge in the field of real estate marketing. A few inquiries of friends or acquaintances who are in the business should help you decide whether such an activity will fit your post-retirement plans.

A little research will reveal that there is hardly a shortage of information on the subject. You will find books and materials whose subject matter range from a straightforward presentation on how to become a real estate broker to how to become a millionaire in real estate with no money and little effort. Publications of the latter type are almost always available in one form or another at "Get Rich Quick" seminars. Assuming your interest in making money in real estate marketing is more modest, we will mention here a few of the steps that you must take in order to become a real estate salesperson.

First, your state department of real estate probably has a special hotline over which you may call to receive licensing information. Such a call should provide you with a large amount of accurate and up-to-date data you will need to make your decision.

You will discover that it is necessary to qualify for a license by passing an examination administered by the state real estate board or commission. Prior to taking the examination, it is advisable to take a real estate course. Such classes are usually available and held at convenient times at your community college, a private business college or in a university or college extension program.

When you receive your license you are ready to go to

work for a broker. It is wise to seek interviews with several. Since you are not under pressure to find immediate employment you can afford to be selective. You should not become associated with an individual or firm unless their goals and expectations are compatible with your own.

Once an agreement has been reached, some of the larger firms provide a two-week training program for new salespersons in which such skills as using the telephone, writing documents, and effective sales techniques are taught.

The usual brokerage fee for the sale of real estate property is 6 percent, up to half of which is your commission, depending on your employer. Thus, if you sell a home for $100,000 you might expect to receive a minimum of $3,000. However, sales commissions are negotiable and it is possible that you may be able to work out an arrangement whereby you will receive a greater percentage of the fee than normally paid.

Summary

We have tried to emphasize the fact that you have numerous options as to how you may wish to spend your time after you have completed your countdown to retirement, not the least of which is to share your knowledge for pay. Having "paid your dues," you have every right to expect a reasonable fee for any additional services you may choose to render. In fact, an argument can be made that work for which a fee is paid is more likely to be appreciated then work that is rendered free of charge. In any case, if you plan well, your rewards most assuredly will come in multiples.

For example, John M. taught art at a community college for 34 years. Upon retirement he volunteered to restore a faded mural on a wall in the sanctuary of St. Ann's Church. The word soon spread about the excellent job he had done. When people who had paintings needing restoration began requesting his services, he discovered that there was a market for his skills that he had not anticipated. He also discovered that receiving payment for work which he enjoyed, which brought satisfaction to his clients, meant that he was receiving triple compensation.

13 *Have Fun*

Conventional wisdom dictates that the retired educator will spend time on the golf course. Many do. Golf is a wonderful activity. It combines exercise and challenge. It can be as demanding or as relaxing as the individual player desires. But golf is not the only sport open to retired educators.

Sports

Tennis, bowling, softball, swimming, archery, basketball, volleyball, handball, racquetball, fishing, sailing, surfing—the chances are if the sport exists, some retired educator is participating in it. No one should feel that the door to active participation in a sport is closed upon retirement from work. On the contrary, for those who choose to be active, that is the day when the door of opportunity opens widest.

If you have not been active in a sport previously, choose one that fits your particular interest and stamina. You won't make the major leagues but you will have something to do when you get up in the morning. Many activities can be continued as long as there is breath in the body. No avid fisherman was ever deterred by age. He might give up trout fishing in remote mountain streams but he substitutes pier fishing, pond fishing or other easily reached fishing opportunities.

The baseball enthusiast may have to give up softball eventually but replaces active participation with enthusiastic participation as a spectator at games.

The key to sport as a way to keep body and mind active is to enjoy sport on either a participant or spectator basis. Televised games are the least desirable substitute for participation. The true sportsman is learning, training, participating all of the time. He is not a passive spectator.

While you are considering which sport you wish to participate in, do some field research. Go to the park on a weekday. Who is on the baseball diamond? Who is on the tennis courts? Who is playing at lawn bowling? Who is practicing archery?

Go to the lake or shore on a weekday. Who is sailing, surfing, swimming, diving, or fishing? Check the bowling alleys, not on a weekend, but on a weekday. Who is bowling? Check the YMCA. Who is working out? Who is swimming? Who is playing handball?

Go to the golf course, not on a Wednesday afternoon, when the doctors, dentists and attorneys are hard at play, but on Monday morning. Who is playing?

By the time you have checked all the venues, you will have convinced yourself that age is no barrier to enjoyment of any sports activities. Go ahead and take your pick of activities and enjoy yourself. Play is therapeutic. You need not feel guilty about wasting time.

Hobbies

Doing something you enjoy every day will add years to your life. It will also add immeasurably to the quality of those added years. A hobby is something you do for fun. It may be bird watching or flying. It may be stamp collecting or letter writing. It may be cooking or eating. Whatever you choose be certain that you do it with zeal. When a hobby becomes a chore, a taskmaster, drop it and find something new to enjoy.

Collecting is a generic term for everything from antiques to zoological specimens. Collecting satisfies an educator's need to learn. You cannot collect without becoming knowledgeable about your subject. No matter what the field, the collector will find friends and material to expand his database.

Paul A. collected ancestors. He traced his genealogy back to the 15th century. He found that each generation he located added to his knowledge of history, of geography, of sociology, of economics. He traveled extensively both in the United States and Europe finding the places his ancestors had lived, discovering their occupations, their reason for moving on. Before long he could appreciate the history of man since 1450 because that history had personal meaning for him.

Marshall McV. collects diatoms, a kind of algae. As a science teacher, Marshall became fascinated by the fact that diatoms have silicon shells which come in many shapes with fine surface sculpturing. Upon retirement he set out to find as many different shapes as he could. Since diatoms are abundant in marine and fresh water, every geographical location on earth provides a potential opportunity to find a new shape. "It's like collecting snowflakes, only diatoms don't melt," Marshall says.

Avis Y. collects early American toys. She searches estate sales, flea markets, and antique fairs to find authentic examples of handcrafted playthings. She reads extensively, travels widely, and searches diligently for clues to those things which entertained children in the time when there was neither television nor national media to promote the standardization of children's toys. Every day Anita has something challenging to do to further her collection.

Collecting is only one of hundreds of hobbies open to those with time to pursue them.

Some retired educators find a welcome change of pace in making things by hand. Some do woodworking, some do needlecrafts, some handweaving. Others make ceramic objects or paint. Some arrange flowers, others grow them. Some make beer or wine. Others do gourmet cooking.

Many retired educators find pleasure in studying a subject of particular interest to them. They may spend time studying in depth the works of some famous author. Some may become experts in the field of local history. Others may live not in the past but in the future, becoming knowledgeable about the cutting edge of technology. Those futurists are among the growing number of older Americans who are racing to outstrip youngsters as computer experts.

Of course many retired educators are to be found among those who have as their hobbies the traditional pursuits of gardening, hunting, fishing, reading and/ or traveling.

The important thing about hobbies is that pursuing an avocation with the same diligence with which you pursued your vocation keeps your mind alive. A brain constantly stimulated stays young. Look about you at the retired persons you know who are in their 80s and 90s. The alert, active individuals in that group are not sitting in rocking chairs waiting to die. They are living every minute of every day.

An example of this zest for life is a charming couple who recently celebrated their 95th birthdays—Annie and Roger L. They are active in politics, in music circles, and in support of education. But that is not their whole life. Annie is still a champion pool player and Roger plays a mean game of bridge. They have been retired from teaching for 30 years but they are still learning.

Travel

"What are you going to do when you retire?" is the question most frequently asked of the about-to-retire person. "Travel" is the almost universal answer.

Many dream of traveling leisurely to some distant place, of staying long enough to see all that is of interest. Some realize the dream. Others, through fear of the unknown, do not.

Earlier we discussed travel in connection with learning opportunities. Now it is time to consider travel for recreation.

Educators, because they have longer vacations than most professionals, travel more extensively before retirement. Travel in every sense is part of the continuing education of the educator. Nevertheless, retirement offers opportunities for a wider range of destinations. It offers opportunities for less expensive travel. It offers opportunities for different experiences.

Once you retire, recreational travel becomes more spontaneous. You can go when the whim strikes you to see spring wild flowers in the desert, to see the whales migrate along the Pacific coast, to follow autumn foliage from Vermont to Virginia. You can explore the countryside around your home. You can visit local tourist attractions when no tourists are around. You can explore places that you had no time to visit previously. Spontaneous, spur of the moment travel underscores the main delight of retirement. You are free. You are free to enjoy life. You are free to make your own decisions about how you spend your time.

Paradoxically, retirement gives you the time to plan your travel so that you obtain maximum enjoyment from the money you spend.

The best trips take nearly a year—nine months of preparation, two months of travel.

Preparation

Preparation for a journey encompasses more than planning an itinerary, deciding among alternative means of transportation, and arranging the practical details. Preparation means knowing all that you can about your destination. History, architecture, geography, culture, customs, holidays, and language all make up background information which transforms you from a tourist into a traveler.

No one should see London without familiarity with Samuel Pepys, Charles Dickens, and other English writers. Spain without *Don Quixote*, France without *Travels With A Donkey*, Germany without *Buddenbrooks* stored in your mental data bank would lack something. No one should visit Ireland without an appreciation of the history of "the troubles." Scotland without knowledge of its battles, its romances and its poetry is just a lot of beautiful scenery. Cromwell, Napoleon, Bismark, Garibaldi, Eisenhower, Montgomery, Rommel, Hitler all have altered the course of European history. When you know what they did and why, you have greater appreciation of what has happened to the countries you are visiting. The names mentioned above are merely a few of the many writers, rulers, and military leaders with whom you really should become acquainted.

Your trip, whether to New England or the United Kingdom, to New Mexico or old Mexico, should start at your local library. Don't limit your pre-travel exploration to history books, geography books and travel magazines. These will give you the public face of the country you are going to visit. Read the novels written by the country's authors. Read the biographies of its famous people to learn about the private lives of people who live in that country. Dig as deeply as you can into the country's past and present. Immerse yourself in things British, French, German—wherever it is you are planning to go.

Sign up for language classes at your local adult education center, community college or university extension program. Learn from cassettes if no other class is available. Learn a basic vocabulary if you are not already fluent in the language of the country you plan to visit.

Exhaust the entries in the library card catalog under the name of the country, description and travel. Read the old books as well as the new. You will have a better appreciation of changes which have taken place over the years.

While you are doing your pre-trip homework don't overlook the tourist authority of the country you are planning to visit. Almost every major country has such an office somewhere in the United States. You will find addresses listed in guide books such as those published by Fodor or Frommer.

The United States government has information available at little or no cost on travel, both foreign and domestic. You might not think of the federal government as a source of travel information, but consider the following:

• *Your Trip Abroad—Travel Tips For Senior Citizens* available from Public Affairs, Bureau of Consular Affairs, Department of State, 2201 C Street N.W., Room 6811, Washington, D.C. 20520.

• *Travel Advisories* (name of country) available from Overseas Citizens Services, Bureau of Consular Affairs, Department of State, 2201 C Street N.W., Room 4800, Washington, D.C. 20520.

While you are writing for the above publications ask the bureau for any other information available concerning the country you plan to visit.

Federal government publications about destinations within the United States are many and varied. You will find them listed under various department and agency headings in *Information U.S.A.* written by Matthew Lesko, Viking Press, N.Y.

Your library is an excellent source of information concerning travel in the United States. Again, read the books listed under the city or state name, description and travel. Don't overlook the wonderful books written by the WPA Writer's Project in the 1930s. Find novels which use the city you will visit as the settings for the stories. Read books about the history and geography of the area. Check books about any particular interest or hobby you have. Glass collectors would not want to visit Cape Cod and miss the Sandwich Glass Museum. There are many little known places of interest to those who specialize in particular fields. You find them only through diligent research. Once located, they add extra enjoyment to your travels.

Most states have tourist information agencies. All large cities have visitor and convention bureaus. Letters to these offices will stimulate a flow of information of all kinds. You will hear from more hotels and motels than you want. Some have special rates which are quite attractive.

Members of the AARP/NRTA can take advantage of the travel assistance provided by that organization.

Visitors to Washington, D.C., should write to their congressman for information and passes to visit the house and senate galleries, the White House, the Library of Congress, and the Department of State diplomatic reception rooms.

Preparation over the months before you travel serves two purposes. First, it will make it possible for you to shed the great cloak of ignorance so many tourists use to insulate themselves from new experiences. Second, it will assist you to save money.

Imagination

Thelma traveled every summer between school terms. When she retired from teaching she was a veteran explorer. She took with her one small carry-on bag and as much money as she could afford. When her clothes became soiled she either found a laundromat or bought replacements in local outdoor markets. She stayed in pensions, furnished rooms or bed-and-breakfast accommodations.

She made her headquarters in a central location in the country outside of major cities and used local transportation to travel about. Thelma never saw more than one part of a country on any one trip. What she saw, she saw in depth. She made friends with every youngster who would speak to her. The children were delighted to have an opportunity to practice English and Thelma had a chance to practice their language on an uncritical audience. She met many families through her contacts with youngsters.

Thelma never carried an ounce of excess baggage, literally or figuratively. She traveled with an open mind and an open heart. When she retired, she continued to travel the same way. The only difference was after retirement she stayed longer and went during fall, winter and spring months—seasons she never before had experienced.

Thelma M. exemplifies the adventuresome traveler.

A plane ticket and money were all she needed. Everything was strictly without plan. She stayed in each area as long as she wished. She saw 10 countries not in 15 days but in 15 years.

Not everyone wants to travel as Thelma did. Nevertheless, we can all learn from her experience.

Money Saving Tips

Are you over 65? You are fortunate if the answer is yes.

We discussed earlier in Chapter 3 the transportation savings available in the United States for those who qualify as senior citizens. Similar savings on transportation costs are available in other countries. When you write to the Tourist Information Office of the country you plan to visit, ask about discount fares and admission prices for those over 65.

We also discussed the discounts offered by hotel chains to members of the American Association of Retired Persons.

You may reduce both transportation and accommodation costs even though you are not yet 65 through membership in discount travel organizations such as Stand-buys, Ltd. These organizations broker discounted travel opportunities via cruise ships, charter flights and tours that are underbooked. Members must be flexible in their travel plans as most of the opportunities offered require that you leave on fairly short notice.

Be an informed consumer. Whether you are buying discount airfares, tours or cruises be on the alert for dishonest companies. Deal with reputable travel agents. Look for those who claim membership in the American Society of Travel Agents (ASTA). Ask your Better Business Bureau whether any complaints have been filed against the organization offering the travel bargain. Be aware of "bait and switch" tactics. Some firms advertise extremely attractive prices on package deals. When you call to book, the offer is no longer available. They have, however, another more expensive package that they can sell you. Sometimes the pitch is more subtle. You can book the cheaper package if you insist but you won't be satisfied with such cramped quarters, or some other such disclaimer.

Read all travel brochures with a practiced eye. Check for ambiguous statements. Read the fine print. What precisely will you receive for the "all inclusive" price? Learn to spot the offers which are misleading. Compare brochures from various companies. Find the company which seems to be the most honest about what it includes and excludes. Then check with your friends to see if any have had satisfactory experiences with that company.

Read the travel publications which rate tour operators, airlines and cruise ships. One of the best of these is the *International Travel News* (ITN). This publication has a section called, "The World Travelers' Intercom" which is a compilation of letters from readers commenting on hotels, cruise ships, airlines, low cost accommodations, restaurants, and so on. Regular reading of this publication gives you a cross section of opinion regarding what is excellent and what is inferior.

If you cannot find the *International Travel News* at your local library, you may secure a sample copy by writing to:

International Travel News
2120 28th Street
Sacramento, CA 95818.

You can save money in European countries (including Britain and Ireland) by using accommodations in private homes. In England, Ireland and Scotland they call these accommodations "B&Bs" (bed-and-break-fast). On the continent they call such places "pensions." By whatever names, they have two things in common. First, they are much cheaper than hotels, inns or guest houses. Second, you will rarely find a room with a private bath; you must use the facilities down the hall. These establishments are operated by their owners, opening their own homes to travelers. You will become acquainted with some very interesting individuals. People genuinely interested in meeting visitors from other countries run B&Bs. You may find yourself discussing politics, farming, inflation, literature, music, education or any of a number of other topics with your host or hostess. Try doing that with the room clerk at the major hotel in the city center.

You may also secure inexpensive accommodations by choosing a self-catering holiday. You rent an apartment, cottage or flat fully furnished and do your own cooking. Most places offer weekly cleaning service. You make your own bed, do the daily washing up and cleaning. Self-catering holidays permit you to mingle with the local citizens as they go about their daily lives. You shop in the local markets for meat, fish, and vegetables. You may encounter some strange foods or different cuts of meat. Ask the clerk for advice. They enjoy teaching ignorant Americans how to cook. For long stays in one area, cottages or flats are the best way to really know how others live.

Of course, there are disadvantages. Who wants to do on holiday what one does every day at home? On the surface self-catering sounds like work, not play. In actuality it is more like playing a game. Nothing is quite real. Shopping is an adventure. Cooking is an experience you won't soon forget.

Another disadvantage is that you can be just as isolated in a cottage as in a hotel. You don't have a host or hostess hovering over you, concerned about your welfare.

There are advantages, as well. Some people suffer from feelings of confinement after several nights in a hotel room. Many long for private bathrooms after long periods of sharing facilities. In a cottage or flat you have a proper bedroom, living room, bath and kitchen. You eat what you like, prepared the way you like it. You can pack a bag lunch to eat in the park while you are out sightseeing. You can save even more than you can using pensions or B&Bs.

You don't need to take guided tours if you have done your homework. You can travel comfortably and independently because of your preparation. You will save money. You will stay longer. You will enjoy yourself more.

When To Go

You have always traveled during the long summer break. You have never had the opportunity to take an extended holiday at other times of the year. You can now find what you missed in previous years.

September and October are exceptionally good travel periods. The summer tourists have gone home. Accommodations are easier to find and less expensive. Most tourist attractions don't close until mid or late October. The new plays have opened. The regular concert, ballet, and opera seasons have started. The weather is often better than in the summer. There is something about the color and light of fall which makes it an ideal travel period.

December is a wonderful time to enjoy the customs of Christmas in other countries. There is something special about the holiday season that makes strangers more friendly. December, however, may have more days when the things you want to see or do are not available. You may find Christmas week a time when theaters close, transportation is overcrowded or shut down, banks closed and most restaurants either closed or overbooked.

Unless you are going where the weather is warm in January, February and March, it is better to stay by your own fireside. Ski buffs will disagree with that assessment. For the majority of retired people, the first three months of the year are the time to go to Florida, Arizona, Hawaii, Mexico, the Caribbean or the South Pacific.

Frequently overlooked destinations for winter travel are the countries "down under." Australia and New Zealand enjoy summer while we are shivering and shoveling snow.

Australia is as large and varied as the United States. Its climate ranges from moderate to tropical. Its geography ranges from lush to barren. Its government is stable. Best of all, the Australians welcome Americans. If you are a sports enthusiast, Australia is the place for you.

New Zealand is about the same size as California. Composed of two long narrow islands, New Zealand has no areas far from the sea. Its climate ranges from subtropical to cold. The scenery varies from beautiful to spectacular. If you like fjords, New Zealand has them. If you like tranquil farmlands, New Zealand has them. If you like alps, New Zealand has them, as well. It, too, has a stable government and water safe to drink.

New Zealand has an unique system of travel accommodations. You book a motel room and you get a mini-apartment. Scattered throughout the North and South Islands are host farms where you can spend a week or a month (at reasonable rates), eating three or four delicious meals a day, coddled and pampered by charming hosts and hostesses. If you like the simple

177

life, a farm holiday is for you. If you like trout fishing, New Zealand is a paradise on earth.

April and May are usually splendid months to travel. There is never a dull day in spring, even when a sudden rainstorm blows through. Trees and flowers are at their best. The tourist season has not yet begun. The concerts and plays are not yet on summer hiatus . Most seasonal tourist hotels and attractions open during Easter week. Almost every place in the northern hemisphere looks good in April and May.

From June through August the wise retired person stays close to home. These are the months to concentrate on preparation. Leave the overcrowded planes, the overbooked hotels, the crowded beaches and resorts for those who are not yet free.

Epilogue

There are so many things to do after retirement it is difficult to stop citing examples of activities we and others have found enjoyable. All of you who have adequately prepared for "D-day" will find that you have not retired *from* life but *to* living. You will find that, to quote the San Diego EGO program, "Wisdom, knowledge, experience cannot be retired." You will find that retirement is indeed the pot of gold at the end of the rainbow.

When your countdown has come to an end, when you leave work for the last time, we welcome you to your new career. We hope that you enjoy your retirement as much as we are enjoying ours.

Every word that we have written is a distillation of years of happy experience with active retirement. We have yet to discover any personal truth in the myths about retirement. We are confident you will be as fortunate.

Appendix A

Inflation Impact Table

End of yr.	@ 2.0%	@ 2.5%	@3.0%	@3.5%	@4.0%	@4.5%	@5.0%
1	1.020	1.025	1.030	1.035	1.040	1.045	1.050
2	1.040	1.051	1.061	1.071	1.082	1.092	1.103
3	1.061	1.077	1.093	1.109	1.125	1.141	1.158
4	1.082	1.104	1.126	1.148	1.170	1.193	1.216
5	1.104	1.131	1.159	1.188	1.217	1.246	1.276
6	1.126	1.160	1.194	1.229	1.265	1.302	1.340
7	1.149	1.189	1.230	1.272	1.316	1.361	1.407
8	1.172	1.218	1.267	1.317	1.369	1.422	1.477
9	1.195	1.249	1.305	1.363	1.423	1.486	1.551
10	1.219	1.280	1.344	1.411	1.480	1.553	1.629
11	1.243	1.312	1.384	1.460	1.539	1.623	1.710
12	1.268	1.345	1.426	1.511	1.601	1.696	1.796
13	1.294	1.379	1.469	1.564	1.665	1.772	1.886
14	1.319	1.413	1.513	1.619	1.732	1.852	1.980
15	1.346	1.448	1.558	1.675	1.801	1.935	2.079
16	1.373	1.485	1.605	1.734	1.873	2.022	2.183
17	1.400	1.522	1.653	1.795	1.948	2.113	2.292
18	1.428	1.560	1.702	1.857	2.026	2.208	2.407
19	1.457	1.599	1.754	1.923	2.107	2.308	2.527
20	1.486	1.639	1.806	1.990	2.191	2.412	2.653
21	1.516	1.680	1.860	2.059	2.279	2.520	2.786
22	1.546	1.722	1.916	2.132	2.370	2.634	2.925
23	1.577	1.765	1.974	2.206	2.465	2.752	3.072
24	1.608	1.809	2.033	2.283	2.563	2.876	3.225
25	1.641	1.854	2.094	2.363	2.666	3.005	3.386
26	1.673	1.900	2.157	2.446	2.772	3.141	3.556
27	1.707	1.948	2.221	2.532	2.883	3.282	3.733
28	1.741	1.996	2.288	2.620	2.999	3.430	3.920
29	1.776	2.046	2.357	2.712	3.119	3.584	4.116
30	1.811	2.098	2.427	2.807	3.243	3.745	4.322

Refer to Chapter 3

Bibliography

1. *American Association of Retired Persons. *Planning For Retirement* (bibliography). Washington, D.C.: American Association of Retired Persons, 1983.
1. U.S. House of Representatives. Select Committee on Aging. *The Economics Of Aging: A Need For Pre-Retirement Planning.* 98th cong., 1st sess.,1983.
1. U.S. Senate. Special Committee on Aging. *Publications List.* 87th-98th cong., 1961-1984.
1. National Council on the Aging. *Publications.* Washington, D.C.: National Council on the Aging, Inc., 1985.
1. National Gerontology Resource Center. *Introductory Readings in Social Gerontology: A Selective Annotated Bibliography.* Washington, D.C.: AARP National Gerontology Resource Center, 1984.
1. Fowles, Donald G., comp. *A Profile Of Older Americans.* Washington, D.C.: American Association of Retired Persons, 1984.
1. (Institute of Lifetime Learning). *Second Career Opportunities For Older People.* Washington, D.C.: American Association of Retired Persons.
1. *Megel, Carl J. *Planning For Retirement.* Washington, D.C.: American Federation of Teachers, AFL-CIO, 1983.
1. Teachers Insurance and Annuity Association. *An Annotated List of Retirement Preparation Programs and Materials.* New York: Teachers Insurance and Annuities Association, College Retirement Equities Fund, 1982.
3. U.S. Department of Labor, Bureau of Labor Statistics. *Autumn 1981 Urban Family Budgets For Selected Urban Areas.* Washington, D.C.: U.S. Department of Labor, April, 1982.
3. *U.S. House of Representatives. Select Committee on

---

* Books and pamphlets which are particularly useful in retirement planning.

Aging, *A Guide To Planning Your Retirement Finances.* 97th cong., 2d sess.,1982.
3. U. S. Department of Labor, Bureau of Labor Statistics. *Three Budgets For A Retired Couple, Autumn 1981.* Washington, D.C.: U.S. Department of Labor, July, 1982.
6. Peterson, James A. *On Being Alone.* Washington, D.C.: American Association of Retired Persons, 1980.
6. U.S. Department of Health and Human Services. Social Security Administration. *A Woman's Guide To Social Security.* Washington, D.C.: U.S. Government Printing Office, 1984.
6. *U.S. Department of Health and Human Services. Social Security Administration. *Your Social Security Rights And Responsibilities: Retirement And Survivors Benefits.* Washington, D.C.: U.S. Government Printing Office, 1985.
7. U.S. Senate. Special Committee on Aging. *Healthy Elderly Americans: A Federal, State And Personal Partnership.* 98th cong, 2d sess, 1984.
7. National Institutes of Health. *The National Institute On Aging.* Washington, D.C.: U.S. Department of Health and Human Services, 1983.
7. National Gerontology Resource Center. *Retirement Housing: Directories.* Washington, D.C.: AARP National Gerontology Resource Center, 1984.
7. *American Association of Retired Persons. *Healthy Questions.* Washington, D.C.: American Association of Retired Persons in Cooperation with Federal Trade Commission, 1985.
7. Hoath, Patricia A. *Sound Advice.* Washington, D.C.: American Association of Retired Persons.
7. *(American Association of Retired Persons). "AARP Volunteers Advise On HMOs." *Modern Maturity* , April-May, 1985:12

7. (Consumers Union). "Medicare Supplement Insurance." *Consumer Reports*, June 1984: 347-355.
7. *Health Care Financing Administration. *Recent Changes In Medicare.* Washington, D.C.: U.S. Department of Health and Human Services, 1982.
7. *National Association of Insurance Commissioners and Health Care Financing Administration. *Guide To Health Insurance For People With Medicare.* Washington, D.C.: U.S. Department of Health and Human Services, 1984.
7. *Moore, Wayne, ed. *Hospital, Nursing Home, Home Health and Hospice Coverage.* Book 3, *Medicare: Obtaining Your Full Benefits.* Washington, D.C.: Legal Counsel for the Elderly, Inc., 1984.
7. *American Association of Retired Persons. *Information On Medicare And Health Insurance For Older People.* Washington, D.C.: American Association of Retired Persons, 1984.
7. *Center for Human Services. *Using Your Medicines Wisely: A Guide For The Elderly.* Rockville. MD.: National Institute on Drug Abuse.
7. *National Institute in Aging. *Help Yourself To Good Health.* Washington, D.C.: National Institute on Aging in cooperation with Pfizer Pharmaceuticals.
7. Curley, Ann and Elliot Carlson. "Now You See It! Now You Don't!: The Strange Story Of America's Home Health-Care System." *Modern Maturity,* April-May, 1985:33-36.
7. U.S. Senate. Special Committee on Aging. *Sheltering American's Aged: Options For Housing And Services.* 98th cong., 2d sess., 1984.
7. U.S. Senate. Special Committee on Aging. *Long Term Needs Of The Elderly: A Federal-State-Private Partnership.* 98th cong., 2d sess.,1984.
7. (Health Advocacy Services, Program Department.) *The Physician Assignment Survey.* Washington,

D.C.: American Association of Retired Persons.

8. U.S. Senate. Special Committee on Aging. *Rural And Small City Elderly.* 98th cong., 2d sess.,1984.

8. U.S. Senate. Special Committee of Aging. *Crime Against The Elderly.* 98th cong., 2d sess.,1983.

8. *(Criminal Justice Services Program Department.) *How To Spot A Con Artist.* Washington, D.C.: American Association of Retired Persons, 1982.

8. *Powers, Carol. *Your Retirement Anticrime Guide.* Washington, D.C.: American Association of Retired Persons and National Retired Teachers Association, 1978.

8. *American Association of Retired Persons. *How To Write A Wrong.* Washington, D.C.: American Association of Retired Persons in cooperation with the Federal Trade Commission, 1983.

8. *Seaton, Michael. *Your Retirement Driving Guide.* Washington, D.C.: American Association of Retired Persons, 1979.

8. *(Program Department). S*afe Living In Your Mobile Home.* Washington, D.C.: American Association of Retired Persons, 1980.

8. (Consumer Affairs Program Department). *Five Ways To Cut Your Phone Costs.* Washington, D.C.: American Association of Retired Persons.

9. U.S. Senate. Special Committee on Aging. *The Costs Of Employing Older Workers.* 98th cong., 2d sess., 1984.

9. Commons, Dorman, ed. *Proposed Issues Agenda.* Sacramento, CA.: California Commission on the Teaching Profession, 1984.

9. Lomkin, Jack. "The Remarkable Dr. Andrus." *AARP News Bulletin.* Vol. 26, No.4.

9. (Institute of Lifetime Learning and Education Committee Task Force.) *So You Want To Be A Gerontolo-*

gist. Washington, D.C.: American Association of Retired Persons in cooperation with Western Gerontological Society.

9. Schwartz, Henrietta, et al. "Schools As A Workplace. The Realities Of Stress." American Federation of Teachers, Washington, D.C. mimeo.

10. *Cohen, Rebecca A. and James M. Thompson. *How To Get Appointed To A Board Or Commission: A Guide For Older Citizens.* Washington, D.C.: American Association of Retired Persons, 1982.

10. *(Institute of Lifetime Learning). *Museum Opportunities For Older Persons.* Washington, D.C.: American Association of Retired Persons.

10. (Tax Aide Program). *People Helping People.* Washington, D.C.: American Association of Retired Persons, 1984.

10. (Program Department). *Older Volunteers: A Valuable Resource.* Washington, D.C.: American Association of Retired Persons, 1983.

10. U.S. Peace Corps. *Career Opportunities*, Washington, D.C.: U.S. Government Printing Office.

10. U.S. Peace Corps. *Older Americans And The Peace Corps*, Washington, D.C.: U.S. Government Printing Office.

10. ACTION. *The Senior Companion Program.* Washington, D.C.: U.S. Government Printing Office.

General

* Briles, Judith. *The Woman's Guide To Financial Savvy.* New York: St.Martin's Press, 1981

* Miller, Theodore J. *Make Your Money Grow.* Washington, D.C.: Kiplinger Washington Editors, Inc.,1983.

* Hardy, C. Colburn. *Your Guide To A Financially Secure Retirement.* New York: New American Library, 1983.

* Porter, Sylvia. *Sylvia Porter's New Money Book For The 80's* New York: Avon, 1980
* Dunnan, Nancy. *Financial Savvy For Singles*. New York: Rawson Associates, 1983.
* Martorana, R. George. *Your Pension And Your Spouse—The Joint And Survivor Dilemma*. Brookfield, WI: International Foundation of Employee Benefit Plans, 1985.
* Lesko, Matthew. *Information U.S.A.*. New York: The Viking Press, 1984.

Index

Colophon

This book was produced by state-of-the-art electronic microcomputer pagesetting, sometimes referred to as "desktop publishing."

It was created on a Macintosh Plus computer with 20 megabyte hard disk drive.

Text was edited and formatted using Microsoft Word 3.01.

Pages were designed and laid out using Aldus PageMaker 2.0a.

Display initial letters and chapter numerals were created in MacDraw.

Chapter opening pages, display pages, and the back cover were output on a Mergenthaler Linotronic 300.

All other text pages were output on an Apple LaserWriter Plus.

Text was set in 11 point ITC Bookman on 14 points leading, utilizing bold, italic, and bold italic variations.

Book design and editing was by Gene Booth.

Front cover design was created by Leo Bestgen.

Order Form

You can help a colleague begin to prepare for retirement years, or simply get additional copies for yourself, by mailing in this order blank. Add $2.00 shipping and handling for the first book, plus 50 cents for each additional book. Please mail with your check or money order (no cash, please) for the full total amount in U.S. funds.

Mail to:
MOONLIGHT PRESS
Box 994
Westminster CA 92684-0994

Please send me the following:

_____ copies of **Countdown To Retirement For Educators** by Wilson Riles and Jessie Heinzman. Price: $9.95 each.

Total:	$_____
CA residents add 6%	$_____
Shipping & Handling	$_____
Amount Enclosed	$_____

Name:_____

Address:_____

_____

City_____

State_____ Zip_____

196

Kathleen Brooks
on FOREX

A simple approach to trading foreign exchange using fundamental and technical analysis

By Kathleen Brooks

Hh

HARRIMAN HOUSE LTD

3A Penns Road
Petersfield
Hampshire
GU32 2EW
GREAT BRITAIN

Tel: +44 (0)1730 233870
Email: enquiries@harriman-house.com
Website: www.harriman-house.com

First published in Great Britain in 2013

978-0-85719-205-9

British Library Cataloguing in Publication Data
A CIP catalogue record for this book can be obtained from the British Library.

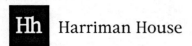

Contents

Acknowledgements

Barry Lane, for his copy editing skills and source of ideas and encouragement. With thanks to Phillip Turner and Nick Slater at BP who first hired me and spent time teaching me the ropes of this market. Lastly, I want to thank all of the retail traders I have met or spoken to. They keep me on my toes and make me strive to improve my research, knowledge and perspective of financial markets and new products.

eBook edition

As a buyer of the print edition of *Kathleen Brooks on Forex* you can now download the eBook edition free of charge to read on an eBook reader, your smartphone or your computer. Simply go to:

http://ebooks.harriman-house.com/kathleenbrooksonFX

or point your smartphone at the QRC below.

You can then register and download your free eBook.

www.harriman-house.com

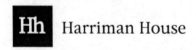 Harriman House

About the author

Kathleen Brooks is a research director for **Forex.com**, a retail FX broker based in London. She uses both fundamental and technical methods in her analysis and fuses the two to get a complete picture of the market.

She is a regular contributor to Yahoo Finance and Reuters Great Debate, and she is often quoted in international publications including the *Wall Street Journal* and the *Financial Times*. She can be seen regularly on business TV including CNBC, Bloomberg, CNBC Arabia, Sky News Australia and the BBC. She started her career in finance at BP where she worked first as a business analyst in its trading division and then as a trading analyst in its foreign exchange dealing room. Prior to joining **Forex.com** she was a financial features writer for *City A.M.*

Kathleen holds an undergraduate degree in English Literature and Classical Civilisation from Trinity College Dublin, and a Master of Science from the Graduate School of Journalism at Columbia University in New York City.

Preface

What this book covers

Since you opened this book then I guess you are interested in foreign exchange, have traded it and want to hone your skills and increase your chances of making a profit. I have been working, learning and trading in foreign exchange for the bulk of my career and over the years I have developed my own philosophy for understanding the largest asset market in the world. It's not your standard approach, but I think that it will strike a chord with traders and that is why I want to share it with you in this book.

There are two main ways of analysing foreign exchange:

1. Using fundamental analysis; and

2. Using technical analysis.

Most people in the markets either look at fundamental analysis *or* technical analysis. But when I first started out in FX, restricting myself to looking at only one of either fundamental and technical factors didn't seem right to me. I always felt that something was missing. These approaches were either way too complex or they were too prescriptive. I wanted something that I could grasp and that made sense to me.

That was when I decided to ditch the dogmatic strategies that pervade the FX market and forge an approach of my own. In the course of my learning about FX I found that I understood the markets best by using neither technical analysis nor fundamental analysis in isolation, but by using them together.

I believe that fundamental factors – politics, economics and even society – cause currency prices to move the way they do (and sometimes in the strangest ways), but throughout the day the smallest price movements are usually based upon technical factors. So you'll get no fundamental or technical purist rhetoric here: my approach is to combine the two. It works for me and I hope by reading about it you'll pick up some ideas for your own trading.

My aim in this book is to teach you my approach to trading the FX market. I assume you already have some knowledge of trading this market – I won't go over the basics, such as giving you an intricate history of a pip, or explaining what a currency cross is. Plenty of pages (both in print and on the web) can give you this information and help you to take your first steps into trading. The website Baby Pips (**www.babypips.com**) is one of my favourites; it provides a great overview for the novice FX trader. Investopedia (**www.investopedia.com**) is another useful resource for an early introduction to the foreign exchange market.

So, rather than presenting you with another *FX 101* I hope to provide a fresh way to view the FX market. This should help you with setting up and executing your trades.

I am a firm believer in learning from observation so this book is packed full of real-life examples and trading set-ups from my recent analysis of the foreign exchange market. Some things deserve a little context or explanation, but I have tried to show more than tell.

The first two parts of this book will look at fundamental and then technical analysis separately before I show you how I combine the two in part C. Part D shows you how I execute my trading strategy in the market using my tried and tested risk management techniques.

Introduction

It was 2006 and I had just joined the forex trading desk at BP as a junior trading analyst. I was a novice, in fact extremely novice, probably the least experienced person that had ever walked on to the BP trading floor. Hence I was not only a young female on a desk full of men but I didn't even have a finance or economics degree. In sum I was totally clueless.

The patience of the traders, the chief dealer and my direct boss, the head of the analytics desk, was amazing. They got me up to scratch on bids and offers, what a pip was and how to trade. They also taught me how fundamentals impact the market. The crossover between central banks, economic data and even politics gripped my imagination and has determined my career path ever since.

In spite of this valuable tuition, when I started out there were a few things I just couldn't understand. Firstly, why was the dollar in such a steep decline? It had been heading south for years against the pound, the yen and the euro. I didn't understand why the dollar would always falter – what about the mean-reversion and efficient markets I had spent months learning about? Also, why did the dollar always seem to fall on *good* economic news out of the US?

If the currency was a reflection of the state of the economy then the US must be in deep economic trouble. But back then growth in America was quite strong and the financial crisis was still ahead of us.

Hence I would write long treatises about how oversold the dollar was, but I could never make a winning trade. I grasped economics and the markets fairly quickly, but something wasn't right. The dollar continued to go against me and I wanted to know why. That was when I learned a bit more theory about the importance of central banks, relative interest rate strategies, changing global growth dynamics and the concept of the safe haven.

As intelligent as I thought all of this new knowledge made me sound, I quickly realised that every time I thought the signals pointed to a stronger dollar, it weakened, and vice versa. Was this market nuts, or should I just give up the challenge of trying to teach myself something I knew nothing about and go and work in something more suited to my academic background?

Luckily I stuck with it and after some time I started to grasp that although you could be *fundamentally* right, you could be *technically* wrong. That was when it clicked; you need to use technical analysis too.

Back to my desk at BP, the guy I sat next to was always trying to show off his technical analysis skills and used fancy words that he knew would confuse me. I kept looking over his shoulder and eventually picked up a few terms the technicians like to throw about: support, resistance, MACD (and no, it's not a burger), RSI and Fibonacci. This last point solidified my affection for the FX market. Fibonacci numbers may have been *discovered* by man but they are derived from nature and this resonated with me. There is a magical, almost mystical, side to how financial markets move, hence price movements tend to follow patterns in nature, and that was a major comfort to me.

Try as I might though, I could only get interested in a few of the elements of technical analysis. Too many lines on the chart, with bull and bear flags popping up every few minutes, left me blurry eyed. While I started to appreciate the benefits of technical analysis I needed something more. That was when it came to me – you can't trade just on the fundamentals or the technicals, you need to fuse them. It seemed to me that the medium-term direction of a cross was down to the fundamentals but the day-to-day price moves, or intra-daily price moves, were all down to technicals.

I decided to stop trying to do what I thought I should do and start doing what I enjoy. I decided to concentrate on the fundamentals and combine them with my favourite technical indicators. That was a match made in heaven for me. That's not to say that I became the most profitable trader in the world, but instead I started to enjoy what I was doing and felt more in control. Hence the birth of my forex philosophy.

After a spell away from foreign exchange and back at graduate school (still not economics, instead journalism) I re-entered the retail FX market a few years back. This has given me the chance to further refine my forex trading approach, which is what I will share with you.

Thank you for reading.

Kathleen Brooks, London, 2013

PART A

Fundamental Analysis

INTRODUCTION

The term *fundamental analysis* is very widely used, but what does it actually mean? The definition of *fundamental* includes:

The foundation or base, forming an essential component of a system and something of great importance.

There are also musical, religious and scientific definitions of fundamental but its definition in relation to the FX market is quite specific – it is the study of the underlying factors that drive a currency's price. In the FX market these underlying factors include the economy, central banks and politics.

We use fundamental analysis in the forex market to help us answer a few basic questions related to these factors, for example:

1. Which economies in the world are growing?

2. Is the growth healthy and sustainable?

3. What are governments and central banks doing to manage their economies?

4. What is the political situation?

The forex trader making use of fundamental analysis takes the answers to these questions and applies them to the decisions they make when placing a trade in the forex market. To explain how this is done I will work through some real-life examples of how to trade using fundamental analysis later in the book.

TRADING USING ECONOMIC DATA

The way to get the information needed for fundamental analysis is to look at the official economic data releases. For most of the world's major economies, economic data is released regularly and it gives a glimpse of the overall economy and how fast it is growing. The key thing for me is that economic growth means future prosperity, which should then equate to a strengthening currency. Traders seek out growth because that is usually where the best opportunities lie to jump on an uptrend. Alternatively, economic data showing weakness in a country's economy has the effect of weakening the currency.

The markets have a tendency to *price in* future growth and prosperity. The forex market, like the stock market, is thought to price in future growth expectations up to six months in advance. Hence markets don't wait for the GDP release that comes out every three months before deciding on the direction of a currency; they react to the incremental flow of data from economic indicators throughout the month in anticipation of what that means for GDP and the overall health of the economy.

In addition to GDP the other indicators include inflation data, retail sales, industrial and manufacturing data, and data on consumer confidence. These are a timely update on the state of the economy and the occasions of their release can be major market-moving events.

In fact, there are thousands of economic indicators and it could make you dizzy if you tried to analyse them all and determine what they mean for growth. As an example of some of the kookier ways of measuring economic growth, some people may look at the hog market to try and detect Chinese consumption of pork and use that to deduce the strength of the Chinese economy. Others have been known to search out demand for a certain chemical found in paint and then try to apply that to demand for housing in the US.

Thankfully there are more accessible ways to understand what is going on from an economic perspective and for some people it is most effective to narrow the list down to a few key indicators. It is also possible to prioritise the indicators so that you can organise your analysis and know which to pay most attention to. I will now move on to introduce the economic indicators that I have found to be of most use in my own fundamental analysis. Before I do, a couple of words on finding economic data.

Use of an economic calendar

It is important to know when economic data is released and the easiest way to get this information is by using a calendar. You can get reliable up-to-date calendars on economic news websites like Bloomberg (**www.bloomberg.com/markets/economic-calendar**), some blogs have them – like Forex Factory (**www.forexfactory.com**), and the financial press often prints economic calendars at the start of each week. Also, ask your FX broker as they may provide you with a free calendar. Some even contain widgets that let you place orders or trade directly from the calendar.

Consensus

The key thing for traders to remember is that the actual data that comes out is only relevant based on whether it hits, misses or exceeds *consensus*. Consensus is an important word for the markets. Usually economic data calendars include the market's expectation of the data release. The *expected* number is the mean of estimates from a number of economists who have been polled prior to the event and asked to give their views on what the number will be. Reuters and Bloomberg are some of the most popular data providers that measure the *street's* expectations prior to major data releases.

As a general rule, a data miss (the figures released are worse than the forecasts) can be currency negative, a number around expectations usually has a negligible effect, and if the reading exceeds expectations this tends to be currency positive.

ECONOMIC INDICATORS

In this section I introduce the four major fundamental indicators that I use to assess the forex market. These are:

1. Labour market surveys

2. Purchasing Managers Index (PMI) surveys and Institute for Supply Management (ISM) surveys

3. Inflation data

4. Quarterly GDP

For each I explain what the indicator is, when it is released, why it is significant and give examples of how it can be used.

1. Labour market surveys

WHAT IS IT?

Without a shadow of a doubt the most important economic statistic for me is the US nonfarm payrolls (NFP) report. It is published by The Bureau of Labor Statistics and measures the number of jobs created in the nonfarm sector of the US economy each month.

WHEN IS NFP DATA RELEASED?

The first Friday of every month.

WHY IS NFP DATA SIGNIFICANT?

American labour market statistics are important because they give an idea about the confidence of American businesses for the future. If a company believes growth will be strong for their product or service going forward they will hire more workers to meet the expected increase in demand. If they think demand is going to contract they will reduce their employee numbers.

Hiring by firms also has an impact on consumer confidence. If people have stable jobs then consumer confidence should be high and they will spend money, whereas if people are losing their jobs the first thing they usually do is cut their spending. Since consumption makes up 70% of the US economy (a level that is far from unique in the West) and jobs are a key component of whether or not consumers are spending, you can understand why the market is so obsessed by this indicator.

NFP data has an enormous impact on all financial markets. Currencies can move more than they customarily would on any normal day and it's not unusual for the major dollar crosses to move a couple of hundred pips in either direction. Stock markets across the globe are also on high alert. Due to the huge amount of volatility that this data can generate, many traders in Asia and Australia stay awake or get up in the middle of the night to place a trade.

FX MARKET EXAMPLE

Lots of people trade before, during and after nonfarm payrolls, and for some of the major FX brokers it can be their busiest day of the month. But I will let you in on my secret: I don't trade the NFP release.

A colleague of mine used to sit patiently looking at his Bloomberg terminal on NFP Friday, as the payrolls report is called by the *street*, and when the number was released he looked at it, digested it and went about doing something else. He chose not to trade the actual figure itself.

This is an important lesson to all traders – economic data like the NFP can produce extremely volatile movement in the markets so some people prefer to wait for the dust to settle and trade when they have a better idea of what effect the NFP data has had. I follow this strategy (or non-strategy) over an NFP release.

Figure 1.1 shows you how volatile the immediate aftermath of an NFP release can be. I have chosen to show the impact the August 2012 data (released on 6 September) had on EURUSD, but it has a similar effect on USDJPY, AUDUSD, GBPUSD, etc. This was the EURUSD's initial reaction to a disappointing payrolls number; the forecast was for a 130k gain in the number of jobs created, but the reality was that only 96k were created and this was considered a disappointment.

The data was released at 13.30 BST and the initial reaction was that the euro sold off sharply, dropping from 1.2650 to 1.2590 in a matter of seconds. It then meandered lower to 1.2570 before rebounding strongly to 1.2650 – back to where it started! – before the end of the London session. This shows you how erratic the market can be during this data release.

There are many reasons why the market can be so erratic on NFP Friday. Firstly, NFPs are one of the earliest releases each month and they are a bit like a new piece of the US economic jigsaw. Since the economy in the US is a complex beast, new information about its strength or weakness can cause shock waves in the financial markets, particularly the FX market. Secondly, hundreds of billions, if not trillions, are being traded during the release, which also causes excess volatility.

Figure 1.1: EURUSD on NFP Friday (6 September 2012)

In the above example it would have been so easy to get caught on the wrong side of that trade. NFP data can be particularly hard to predict so rather than take a bet on whether the number will beat or miss expectations, I wait it out.

Instead my trading strategy for NFPs is more long term. I do two things immediately after the NFP release:

1. Digest what the data is showing; and

2. Decide if that is good or bad for the future trajectory of EURUSD.

On this occasion the data miss was extremely significant as it rounded off a week of bad economic data from the US. This data added to the body of evidence that the US economy was slowing down and would need some help from the US central bank to get going again (see the interest rate section for more).

Since central bank stimulus in the past has been dollar negative, I decided to put on a long EURUSD trade at 1.2650. Some may argue that I bought at the high of the day – how can that be a good trade!? – but in Figure 1.2 you will see that EURUSD rallied a staggering 400 points in the week after the NFP data was released. The circled area shows where I entered the trade, on 6 September 2012.

Figure 1.2: EURUSD (6 September to 21 September 2012)

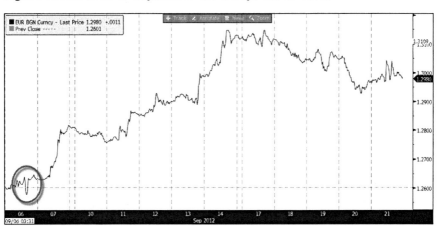

2. Purchasing Managers Index (PMI) and Institute of Supply Management (ISM) surveys

WHAT IS IT?

Purchasing Managers Index (PMI) surveys in Europe and China, and Institute of Supply Management (ISM) surveys in the US, are arguably the second most important pieces of economic data after NFPs.

They are useful for the currency trader for a couple of reasons. Firstly, they are used around the world and are not just US centric like payrolls, thus they can be a good gauge of global growth. Secondly, they are a snapshot of business sentiment in a wide variety of areas like exports, new orders and inventory levels. The results can be used to predict hiring patterns and also the strength of consumer demand.

PMI and ISM surveys originally focused on the manufacturing sector but as the manufacturing surveys evolved and grew in popularity they have expanded to the services and construction sectors. Each country's PMI survey polls hundreds of domestic businesses on the level of new orders they have received, order backlogs, shipment orders, the prices they pay for materials, employment, new export orders and imports.

In the euro zone the fusion PMI Composite index is an important indicator of the overall performance of the currency bloc's economy.

These surveys are conducted around the middle of the month before the data is released. The result is a diffusion index that measures expansion or contraction in service and manufacturing businesses. These indexes have values between 0 and 100, with 50 acting as the line between expansion and contraction. A strong release is above 50, a weak result is below 50.

WHEN IS THE DATA RELEASED?

Usually the first week of every month (the exact day depends on each country). China and Europe do things differently and release first and second readings of their PMI surveys. The first reading is usually the third week of the survey month; the second reading usually takes place the first week of the next month. However, check your economic calendar as sometimes the timings can differ.

WHY ARE THEY SIGNIFICANT?

These surveys tend to have a close relationship with GDP data and are a timely signal of the growth (or lack of) in an economy. As I mentioned at the start of the chapter, the currency trader is always looking for where growth is strong and also where it is weak in order to find the best opportunities to go long or short a currency. ISM and PMI surveys provide this information.

FX MARKET EXAMPLE

The actual PMI and ISM data releases can be good economic data to trade, in contrast to payrolls. For my part, I find it easier to read them. The index is either strong (above 50) or weak (below 50). Revisions are only relevant for the euro zone and China and they tend to be small, thus this is a well-respected and reliable gauge of economic strength or weakness.

When I trade the actual data release I tend to follow these steps:

1. I know what day and time the data is being released.

2. I find out what the market consensus is – does the market expect a strong or weak release?

3. I come up with a trade plan. A number around consensus may only have a limited impact on the market; it's the outliers that tend to have the capacity to change trend. I find out the current trading range and look for support and resistance levels (see technical analysis chapter) that could double up as breakout zones. I may leave a buy order at the top of the range and a sell order at the bottom of the range just in case an outlier causes the cross to change trend.

4. At the time of the release I digest the number and make changes to my orders if necessary. Your broker should allow you to change orders without a charge.

A NEGATIVE SURPRISE IN EURO ZONE PMI DATA

Figure 1.3 shows EURUSD after the release of a weak preliminary reading of the September 2012 PMI data. The survey was below 50, which dashed hopes that the euro zone's struggling economy was starting to recover. This weighed heavily on EURUSD. As you can see this cross fell from 1.3040 all the way to 1.2920 in the aftermath of the news.

Although the euro recovered some of the losses during the next day's trading, this data is significant for the direction of the euro in the long term. The continued weakness in the euro zone economy could make some traders think twice before they put on a long euro trade in the coming weeks as the economic fundamentals look too weak to support the currency at a higher level.

Figure 1.3: EURUSD (20 September 2012)

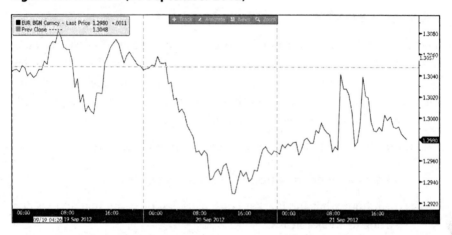

GBP is also sensitive to PMI data releases. Let's take a closer look at the UK's October manufacturing PMI release on 1 November 2012. There are two ways to trade this piece of data:

1. Trade the data release itself, or

2. Wait to digest the data and then make your move.

Here is a trade set-up for trading the actual data release.

1. Homework: growth had been strong in the third quarter but the signs suggested that October had been weak and the strong performance could not be matched. Thus, there was a growing fear that the data may be even lower than broad expectations. Indeed, as it happened the data was weaker than expected for October as it came in at 48.4, whereas the market had expected a reading of 49.0. Also important to bear in mind was that GBPUSD had traded higher in the second half of October.

2. A data miss is likely to weigh on GBPUSD, so a sell order could be left around 1.6100 to benefit from this. As you can see in Figure 1.4, GBPUSD sold off sharply in the immediate days after the October PMI data miss.

Figure 1.4: GBPUSD short-term chart

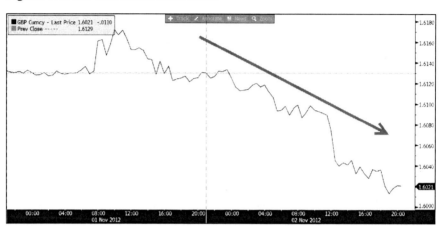

Remember that trading around the data release can be volatile and extra risky, so this is usually a short-term strategy. A longer-term trader may prefer to trade once they have digested the release. However, in this example that would have only been profitable for a couple of weeks. In mid-November market sentiment shifted as risky currencies like the pound started to rally and the trend changed (see Figure 1.5).

Figure 1.5: GBPUSD 1-month chart

3. Inflation data

WHAT IS INFLATION DATA?

Inflation is an important part of a country's economic picture. Fundamental traders should always know what direction inflation data is moving and the pace of change for the economies of the currencies they are trading.

There are two types of inflation to look out for: *CPI (consumer price index)* data and also *PPI (producer price index)* data. The CPI data measures price changes paid by the consumer at the supermarket, shopping centre, etc. The PPI data measures the change in prices of items as they leave the factory gate.

There are also two components to the inflation picture to be aware of: headline and core prices. Headline inflation includes the price of food and energy, while core inflation strips food and energy prices out. Some central banks prefer to focus on the core measure as it is considered more stable. This is because energy and food prices can be extremely volatile – for example, the price of corn or vegetables can be impacted by a freak weather pattern that causes their price to soar one month over the next. This could cause a big spike in headline inflation, but it is likely to be a temporary phenomenon (hence the volatility).

Central banks don't want to change the direction of monetary policy based on a single factor affecting the price of corn, or any lone item, so they look at the core inflation rate instead, which is considered to be a smoother measure of price changes and trends in the economy.

WHEN IS INFLATION DATA RELEASED?

Inflation data is usually released in the middle of each month, but it does depend on the country. The euro zone, UK, US and China tend to release inflation data monthly, while Australia and New Zealand release it quarterly.

Be sure to consult an economic data calendar so that you know the date and time of these releases.

WHY IS INFLATION DATA SIGNIFICANT?

Changes in price data are an important way to determine the state of the economy. Usually falling prices mean that activity is slowing, which can be currency negative, while rising prices can mean that the economy is expanding, which can be good news for a currency.

Inflation data becomes interesting when it gets to extreme levels. So if a country's prices are deemed to be rising too fast it may cause the central bank of that country to adapt its policy to try to get the prices back under control. Central banks like steady increases in prices, and if prices rise or fall too quickly they usually react. This can have implications for the direction of currencies (see the section on interest rates to find out more).

FX MARKET EXAMPLES

EXAMPLE 1: US INFLATION AND USDJPY

While a single inflation data point may not be a major market moving event, its change over time can have huge implications for monetary policy and thus the direction of a currency. Figure 1.6 for the period late 2010 to summer 2012 shows core inflation in the US and also USDJPY. As you can see, as inflation rises it tends to mean a strong USDJPY rate. In contrast, when inflation started to fall in spring 2012 it dragged USDJPY down with it.

The trend in inflation does not follow the currency cross perfectly, as you can see in this chart, so this data point is better for the long-term trader with a multi-month view. If you are a short-term trader, make sure you keep up to speed with inflation data and which direction it is going, but it will be harder (if not impossible) for you to trade off inflation data alone.

Figure 1.6: US inflation and USDJPY (late 2010 to summer 2012)

15

EXAMPLE 2: CHINESE INFLATION AND AUDUSD

From April 2012 to November 2012 the Chinese inflation rate started to decline. This decline accelerated from July 2012. Declining inflation can be bad for a currency as it can suggest that the economy is slowing down. China does not have a free-floating exchange rate, so domestic economic data does not have a huge impact on the renminbi. However, the Aussie dollar has close trade links with China, and signs that growth and inflation were slowing in its important trade partner initially weighed on the AUDUSD, as you can see in Figure 1.7.

The Aussie sold off sharply from April to the end of May as the market digested signs of a Chinese slowdown. However, after that the Aussie recovered, but it didn't manage to break above a key resistance level of 1.06. Thus, although the relationship between AUDUSD and Chinese data is not perfect, Aussie gains were capped while Chinese data remained subdued.

Figure 1.7: AUDUSD daily chart (April to November 2012)

Inflation data is also useful for trading other fundamental events including central bank meetings and GDP releases. This means that even if I don't want to trade the inflation release itself I usually make a point of keeping an eye on the latest inflation release for currencies I am interested in.

4. Quarterly GDP

WHAT IS IT?

This data is the ultimate snapshot of an economy's health. The technical definition of GDP is the market value of all goods and services produced by a country. It is also considered to be a measure of a country's standard of living.

The measurement of GDP was developed in the US in 1934 and the most common formula is:

GDP = private sector consumption + gross investment + government spending + (exports − imports)

Although it is reported quarterly, the data in the major economies usually includes an annual growth rate, so you can see how the economy performed in the past 12 months.

WHEN IS GDP DATA RELEASED?

GDP is reported quarterly for most countries in the world. Usually a GDP report is released in the first month of a new quarter, but consult an economic calendar to get the exact date and time. Also, there are usually a couple of subsequent revisions to GDP data after the main release, especially in the major economies.

WHY IS GDP SIGNIFICANT?

GDP data tells the story of how an economy performed over a period of time – its change relative to previous quarters gives a good indication of which direction the economy is moving and where it may go in the future. A strong positive reading is good news for an economy, while the opposite is bad news. The annualised data is extremely useful for detecting changes in the economic cycle, which can have big implications for FX markets.

Since GDP data is used to determine a country's position in the economic cycle, it is of use for a longer-term trader. Like inflation data, GDP data is of more limited use for the short-term trader – they would be watching to see if the actual figure exceeds or misses the consensus estimate by a large margin. Usually if GDP data is in line with estimates then it barely moves the FX market.

FX MARKET EXAMPLE

GDP can cause volatility in the FX market if it is wildly different to consensus estimates. Let's look at two examples of data surprises and see how it impacted FX.

EXAMPLE 1: UK

Third quarter UK GDP in 2012 was much stronger than expected, rising 1% versus expectations of a 0.6% rise. This data was even more important than usual since it meant that the UK had exited recession for the first time in 2012. This was difficult to predict, so the better trading strategy, in my view, would be to digest the data and then make your move. This was my strategy:

1. I asked myself what caused the UK to grow so strongly (it ended up being one-off factors like the Olympics and the Jubilee bank holiday, which weren't expected to contribute to growth later in the year).

2. This made me think that GBP strength on the back of this report may be short lived.

3. I wanted to trade the pound, but I had to be clever about it. A long GBP position would most likely only work against a currency where growth is weak. The euro was an obvious candidate. As you can see in Figure 1.8, EURGBP declined 190 basis points in the two weeks after the data release.

Figure 1.8: EURGBP in the immediate aftermath of the UK's Q3 2012 GDP

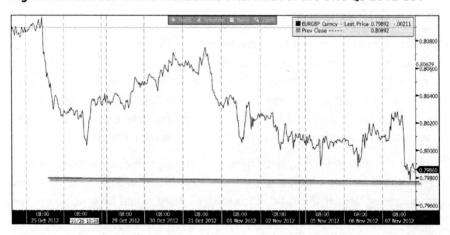

EXAMPLE 2: JAPAN

Japan's economy contracted sharply in the third quarter of 2012, in contrast to the UK. It contracted by 3.5% on an annualised basis in Q3, a sharp slowdown relative to the 0.3% expansion in the second quarter.

Japan's economy was weaker than expected, but rather than cause the yen to sell off, it actually caused the yen to strengthen by 100 pips versus the USD in the immediate aftermath.

How so?

The yen is a safe haven currency and even when there is a negative domestic economic shock it can cause a flight to its perceived safety. However, it would not have paid to remain short USDJPY for long, as you can see in Figure 1.9.

The price action after the data release is circled, but in the following three weeks USDJPY rallied 300 pips. Thus, the rush to the safety of the yen was only temporary, and once the market digested the news the yen reacted as you would expect, and started to weaken.

Figure 1.9: USDJPY – 30-day chart

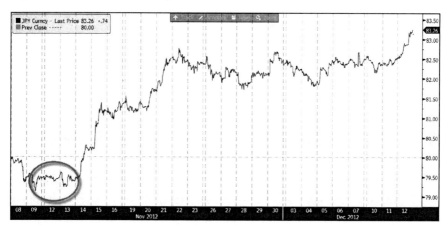

How currencies are affected by the various economic data

Some currencies are more sensitive to particular economic indicators than they are to others. Here is my very quick guide to which major economic data releases affect particular currencies.

- **Euro**: PMI data for the euro zone, inflation data, German factory orders, retail sales and sovereign debt auctions

- **Sterling**: PMI surveys, public sector borrowing figures, retail sales, GDP and GDP revisions. For example, the August 2012 manufacturing PMI survey (released 3 September 2012) beat expectations, causing a sharp jump higher in GBPUSD, as you can see in Figure 1.10. The arrow indicates the point of the data release.

Figure 1.10: GBPUSD (3 September 2012)

- **Australian dollar**: Chinese PMI survey, Chinese GDP projections, domestic terms of trade data and quarterly inflation report (Australia is unusual in that it only releases inflation data every three months). For example, the Australian dollar is extremely sensitive to developments in China because of the close trade links between the two economies. When important Chinese data is released – like GDP – it can have a big impact on the direction of AUDUSD. Figure 1.11 shows how Chinese GDP growth in 2009 came at the same time as a rise in AUDUSD, while moderation in Chinese GDP growth coincided with a slowing rise in AUDUSD in the period from late 2010 to 2012.

Figure 1.11: AUDUSD and Chinese GDP (late 2007 to 2012)

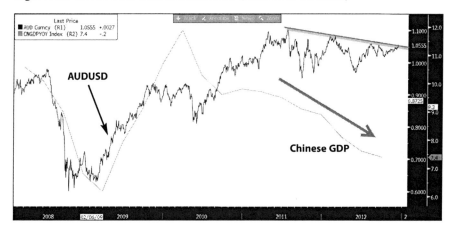

- **US dollar**: NFP, ISM surveys, consumer confidence, retail sales and CPI.
- **Yen**: US NFP, domestic inflation data, the Tenkan survey of manufacturing activity (a quarterly version of the ISM and PMI surveys) and central bank meetings in the US and Japan.

✳ ✳ ✳

I have covered the most important indicators that I believe you need for effective fundamental analysis. Of course there are second, third and even fourth tier indicators that some traders follow avidly; such as terms of trade, factory orders and inventories. However, the purpose of this book is not to give you a step-by-step guide to all economic data because there are plenty of other books that will do that for you.

These include Richard Yamarone's *The Trader's Guide to Key Economic Indicators*, which is an easy to use and comprehensive look at most US economic indicators (but it can be applied to indicators used in other parts of the world).

You may have noticed that I did not include interest rates – and the central banks that set them – in the list of four economic indicators above. I like to think of these as a cousin of the monthly economic data statistics and use them in combination with all of the other indicators. Interest rates have a big impact on the direction of currencies and they are worth looking at in detail, so I will move on to this next.

INTEREST RATES AND CENTRAL BANKS

Central banks control interest rates and interest rates are important for a currency. That is what you should take away from this section of the book. In the following section I will explain what central banks do, show using real-life examples why they are so pivotal to FX and thus why I watch them to inform my trading.

The major central banks

Most countries in the world have a central bank. They tend to meet monthly, or at least seven or eight times a year, to decide policy. The most important central banks in the G10 are:

- US Federal Reserve (Fed)
- European Central Bank (ECB)
- Bank of Japan (BOJ)
- Bank of England (BOE)
- Reserve Bank of Australia (RBA)

The People's Bank of China (PBOC) is also one to watch, even though it does not stick to a rigid timetable to announce policy decisions.

What central banks do

Central bank operations are complex, with a variety of different roles and responsibilities. I am going to give you a simplified version here and then explain what their work means for FX.

Central banks are the government entities involved in controlling a country's money supply; they have the power to take money out of the economy or pump it back in. In doing so, they have a few main tasks:

1. Manage economic growth
2. Keep the currency stable
3. Some central banks also have a mandate to move the workforce towards full employment (the US Fed has this duty).

Essentially central banks monitor the economy. They like nice, steady economic growth and when they see things moving too fast or slow they need to get involved to try and steady the ship.

So, if an economy is growing too fast there will be a fear of overheating. When this happens asset bubbles can form, which tend to pop and then cause recessions. A central bank wants to avoid this. Symptoms of an overheating economy include rising inflation and a fast pace of growth. When they see this the central bank can hike interest rates. By doing this they try to remove some of the heat from the economy by making money more expensive, thus trying to limit investment, cool consumption and cause a managed slowing down.

When central banks raise interest rates they make money more expensive. People prefer to save rather than spend because they earn more on their deposits. The amount of money in circulation tends to fall, which means that the value of money tends to rise.

Let's say the economy starts slowing down sharply, as we saw during the financial crisis in 2008. Back then major central banks around the world cut interest rates as they wanted to make money cheap to disincentivise people from saving, instead encouraging people to spend and invest in the economy to try to boost growth. This means that central banks are putting money back into the system by making it cheap – this increases the money supply and tends to cause the currency to fall in value. In crude terms:

- Central banks raise interest rates = currencies rise
- Central banks cut interest rates = currencies fall

Central banks in action

The trader should always be interested in what the central banker will do next: what will be the next policy decision, will they tighten or loosen interest rates and will currencies go up or down? There are three particular things traders should watch out for when it comes to central banks:

1. *Monetary policy decisions and any press conferences* held by the president or governor of the bank (this is particularly relevant for the ECB and the Fed).

2. *Minutes from central bank meetings,* which give an insight into the thought process behind policy decisions and can be useful for predicting what central banks will do next.

3. Central bankers make *speeches* throughout the year that give an insight into what they are thinking, how they see the economy and what they might decide at the next policy meeting. Economic calendars usually include data for central banks, when bankers are speaking, etc.

There is also a bit of lingo that traders need to be aware of when it comes to central banks:

- **Hawkish**: when central banks are concerned that the economy may be growing too fast and may be about to hike interest rates they are referred to as *hawkish.*

- **Dovish**: when central banks are worried the economy is slowing down too fast and may be about to cut interest rates they are referred to as *dovish.*

So, FX markets are sensitive to changes in monetary policy and also to minutes and speeches from central bankers that give an insight into their thoughts.

Here are a couple of examples of this.

MINUTES FROM THE RBA AND AUDUSD

Figure 1.12 shows AUDUSD in the aftermath of dovish minutes from the RBA's September 2012 meeting in which it sounded worried about economic growth, making a cut in interest rates more likely than a hike.

This caused an immediate dive in the Aussie. The circled area indicates the point of release of the dovish RBA minutes and the impact they had on AUDUSD – it caused the Aussie to sell off for most of the day. If I wanted to trade around the minutes there were a few things that I could do:

1. Check what the market was expecting. In this instance the RBA had left rates on hold in September so the markets expected the minutes to be fairly neutral.

2. Once the minutes had come out and the dovish message had been digested, a short AUDUSD trade could be placed around 1.0470-80 with a target of approximately 60 pips, with a 20 pip stop (see the risk management section for more on trade set ups).

This would have made a nice intra-day trade: the market was taken by surprise by the RBA sounding so concerned about the state of the economy, so placing a short AUD trade could make a small profit. It could also work as a long-term trade, especially if you thought the RBA may cut rates later in the year.

In that case a short position could be entered with a much wider stop and lower profit target. A long-term trade would require more preparation: for example it would be worth looking back over recent economic data from Australia to see if the economic data had started to deteriorate and thus would justify a cut in rates by the RBA.

Figure 1.12: AUDUSD following dovish minutes from the RBA (18 September 2012)

FED MONETARY POLICY AND USDJPY

Some currency pairs are particularly sensitive to central banks' monetary policy. For example, USDJPY is very sensitive to changes in stance by the Federal Reserve. Figure 1.13 shows USDJPY and US Treasury yields. Treasuries (US government debt) tend to move closely with changes in Fed policy and are a good way to gather the market's view on whether the Fed is dovish or hawkish.

Price moves Inverse to yields

BondsV-yields

The first thing to note about government debt is that price moves inverse to yields: so when central banks are hawkish, Treasury bond prices fall and yields rise; and when banks are dovish, Treasury bond prices rise and yields fall. This relates back to the earlier section when I described how central banks control money: when the economy is strong they hike rates, which pushes up interest rates and pushes down the price of debt as fewer investors want to borrow money. When interest rates fall this pushes up the price of debt as more investors want to borrow, but it also pushes down interest rates.

The main thing you should know is this: falling Treasury yields (the Fed is dovish) tends to be dollar negative, while rising Treasury yields (the Fed is hawkish) tends to be dollar positive.

Figure 1.13: 10-Year Treasury yields and USDJPY (2011 and 2012)

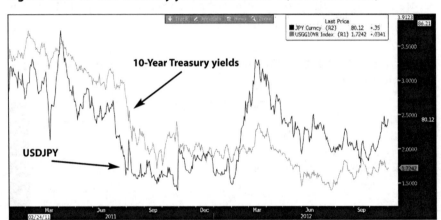

Why is this relationship so close?

US Treasuries are very popular investments to hold and are the most traded government securities in the world. The Japanese are some of the world's largest holders of US government debt, holding nearly 1 trillion dollars' worth. Thus, when Treasury yields fall, as they had been doing since the first quarter of 2012, it means that the price of Treasuries rises. This means that the USD value of Japan's holding of Treasuries rises, and to hedge themselves some Japanese traders start selling USDJPY.

Of course, the forex market is influenced by so many factors it can be hard to claim one group of people cause the movement in a currency cross, however this explanation is well known in the currency markets and I believe it goes some way to explaining the traditionally close relationship between Treasury yields and USDJPY.

Unconventional central banking

In 2012 the pace of global growth had slowed after the recovery from the financial crisis in 2008 had been weaker than expected. Since central banks in the UK, US, Japan and the euro zone had already cut rates to extremely low levels they then had to use unconventional measures to try to boost growth.

This included quantitative easing (QE), whereby the central bank buys government debt to try to depress long-term interest rates and interest rates on mortgages. The Federal Reserve in the US embarked on its third round of QE in September 2012 in another attempt to boost the US economy. This is a largely untested strategy in the history of central banking, and time will tell if it has an effect on the economy.

The intended impact of QE is to limit currency strength; however it depends on how aggressive the central bank is. As you can see in Figure 1.14 – where QE2 and QE3 are circled – the dollar is very sensitive to QE and it tends to lead the currency weaker.

Figure 1.14: Dollar index (the dollar vs. its major trading partners); QE2 and QE3 are circled

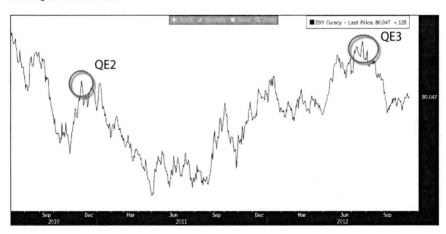

Interest rate differentials

Interest rate differentials are a fairly sophisticated strategy for the retail FX trader, but this is a popular technique with large investment banks and hedge funds so it is worth the retail trader being aware of it so they know how the big guys make decisions in the FX market.

Since two currencies are always traded together and interest rates can determine the value of a currency, a popular trading strategy is to buy a currency with a higher interest rate and sell a currency with a lower interest rate. This is called the *carry trade*.

For example, interest rates in Australia were 3.5% in June 2012; in contrast, US interest rates were at 0%. Due to this, the Aussie dollar was a more attractive currency to hold relative to the dollar. Indeed, this was the case for most of the period from 2010 to 2012 and as a result AUDUSD has been in an uptrend in that time, as you can see in Figure 1.15.

But you will notice that this pair has been extremely volatile, with some large swings up and down. The carry trade is volatile so traders need to be on their guard. Part of the reason for this volatility is that central banks can change policy unexpectedly and their movements can be hard to predict with accuracy.

Figure 1.15: AUDUSD, showing uptrend (2010 to 2012)

Here is another example. Although interest rates in the euro zone in autumn 2012 were higher than they were in the US, EURUSD did not present a good opportunity for the carry trade as the rate differential was only 75 basis points. However, changes in the difference between US Treasuries and German Bunds (using Germany as a benchmark for the entire currency bloc) can impact the direction of EURUSD.

As you can see in Figure 1.16, the difference between German and US bond yields had been trending lower at the start of the year and again from June to October. This means that German bond yields were lower than US bond yields, which weighed on EURUSD.

But how can that be when euro zone interest rates are higher than US interest rates? The currency market can also react to the expected change in rates – thus, as the euro zone economy deteriorated at a faster pace than the US economy in 2012 German bond yields fell, which weighed on EURUSD.

Figure 1.16: EURUSD and the difference between German 10-year bond yields and US 10-year bond yields

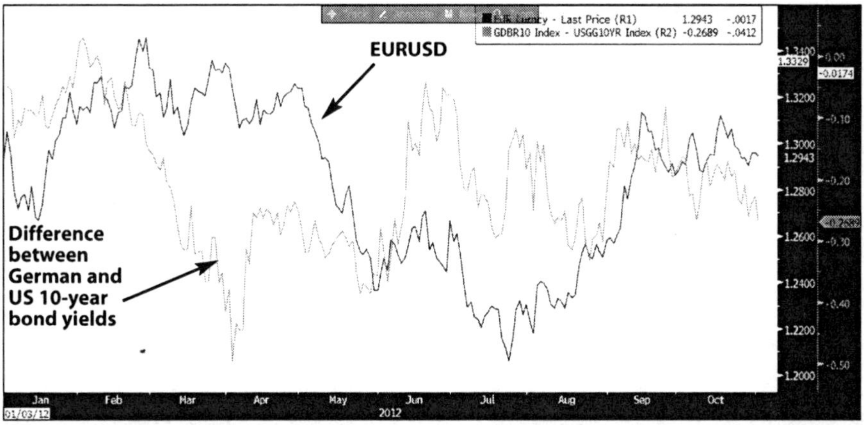

Central bank intervention

As you may have gathered, the US Federal Reserve is the most influential central bank. However, currency traders need to keep an eye on other banks as well.

The Bank of Japan (BOJ) and the Swiss National Bank (SNB) in recent years have directly intervened in the forex market to weaken their currencies and thereby protect their export sectors and boost growth. I will use two examples to show the different effects that central bank intervention can have on the FX market.

1. BANK OF JAPAN INTERVENTION TO WEAKEN THE YEN IN MARCH 2011

The BOJ wanted a weaker currency to stimulate growth in the country after a major tsunami and earthquake caused an economic disaster in March 2011. The BOJ and other central banks decided to sell yen in a multilateral attempt to weaken Japan's currency.

Although the exact amount of yen sold is unknown, it was not enough to keep the yen weak for long. Instead this type of FX intervention was more of a gesture to show solidarity with Japan in its hour of need. This was not deemed aggressive central bank intervention.

As you can see in Figure 1.17 where the timing of central bank intervention has been circled, although USDJPY jumped from 79.00 to 86.00 in a matter of days, it soon started to weaken again.

Figure 1.17: USDJPY (February and March 2011)

2. Aggressive intervention by the SNB

In contrast, the Swiss National Bank (SNB) embarked on an aggressive bout of intervention in August 2011 after EURCHF fell to its lowest ever level. This caused the SNB to worry about Switzerland's export-dominated economy that relies on a weak exchange rate to make its exports competitive.

Thus, the SNB decided to instigate a floor in EURCHF at 1.20. That meant that it would buy EURCHF to ensure that the pair got back to this level and stayed there. The cost was that the SNB had to buy billions of euro, but the upside was that it helped to protect the Swiss economy.

This is extremely aggressive action from a major central bank and is very rare. As you can see in Figure 1.18 – which shows the aftermath of the intervention from December 2011 onwards – the FX market took the SNB's action seriously and EURCHF has barely budged from 1.20 since the floor was put in place.

Figure 1.18: EURCHF (late 2011 and 2012)

POLITICAL RISKS

Politicians control the economy and their policies can change the future growth trajectory of an economy. Political risk that fundamental forex traders need to be aware of comes in a few forms:

1. Changing of governments.

2. When policies change that could affect economic growth.

3. When unexpected circumstances arise that the market had not anticipated.

The key thing to remember with political risk is that traders like certainty – they like to know who is in charge of an economy and that they will take the right decisions to boost economic growth. Thus:

- A low level of political risk tends to be currency positive

- A high level of political risk tends to be currency negative

Greece is a good example of political risk and how high levels of political uncertainty can weigh on a currency. In early 2010 a new government was elected and it uncovered a huge gap in the budget deficit – Greece had been borrowing more than it could afford to pay back and the country was nearly bust. The previous government had covered this up.

This sent the markets into shock and since Greece is part of the euro zone the price of the euro was sent tumbling from 1.45 to below 1.20 by mid-2010 (see Figure 1.19). Not since the end of the Second World War had a Western country defaulted on its debt, and now Greece needed to get financial assistance from its European partners, the International Monetary Fund (IMF) and the ECB to prevent this from happening.

The market's view that the euro zone was stable and therefore a safe investment was shaken to the core. If Greece was in trouble, could it spread elsewhere? Indeed it did and Portugal and Ireland also requested bailouts.

Figure 1.19: EURUSD (2010)

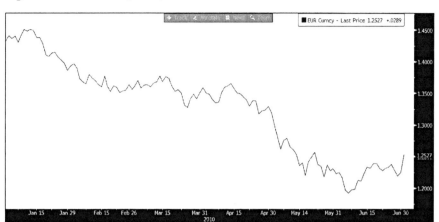

Once a country is labelled as being politically risky it can be a difficult mantle to shake off. In the period April to June 2012 Greece had to hold two elections before the new government came to power. This heightened political risk yet again and also weighed on the euro as the markets fretted that Greece would vote in politicians who did not want to stick to the terms of its bailout loans, which could have seen Greece thrown out of the currency bloc.

Greece eventually did elect a political party who would comply with bailout terms, but this was a difficult period for the euro, as you can see in Figure 1.20. It sold off sharply from 1.34 in March 2012 to 1.24 during the second Greek election in June 2012.

Figure 1.20: EURUSD (2012)

Political instability can cause excess volatility in the FX market. When this happens investors put their money in the safest place possible – such as cash or cash equivalents like Treasury bonds – and sell risky assets that could fall in value.

The concept of safe havens and risky assets

An important trick of the trade in the foreign exchange market is the concept of the safe haven and the risky currency. Traders should acquaint themselves with risky currencies and safe havens since during periods of market panic – such as financial crash, a geopolitical event or a natural disaster – the market tends to divide the currencies into these two groups.

When the market panics there is typically liquidity flow out of risky currencies and into safe havens. Conversely when the markets are stable and growth is good, when there are no financial or geopolitical crises on the horizon and there haven't been any natural disasters, then this can be an environment that allows risky currencies to appreciate.

Both risky and safe currencies can move on domestic factors that have nothing to do with the overall market environment, but when the going gets tough the herd mentality can take over in FX, so domestic fundamentals go out of the window and fear takes over.

THE SAFE HAVENS

Safe havens are the currencies that traders tend to buy in times of distress in the financial markets. Safe haven currencies have certain characteristics:

1. Political stability

2. Financial stability

3. They are usually deep and liquid, which means that they are frequently traded.

The most important safe havens are:

- The US dollar

- The Japanese yen

- The Swiss franc

The US dollar is the ultimate safe haven for a couple of reasons:

1. The US is the world's largest economy and is thus considered stable

2. The US government has never defaulted on its debt.

The dollar is also the most widely owned currency in the world, which makes the dollar attractive to hold in a crisis. If you need money fast you want to own assets that are easy to sell, like the US dollar.

WHAT THIS MEANS FOR FX MARKETS

When panic and uncertainty hit the markets traders want to buy the dollar, which causes it to rise. For example, when Lehman Brothers filed for bankruptcy in September 2008 the dollar sky-rocketed (see Figure 1.21). But how can that be, when Lehman Brothers was an American company? That is the funny thing about the dollar; it can rise even when the problem is the US economy.

Figure 1.21: Dollar index (September 2008 to February 2009)

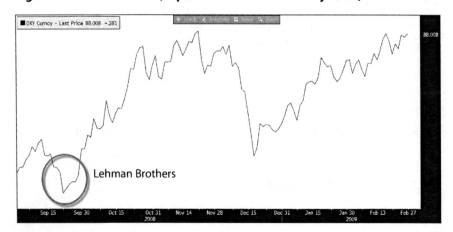

RISKY CURRENCIES

The opposite of a safe haven is a risky currency. This is a currency that tends to sell off in times of market panic. A currency can be classified as risky if it has one or more of the following characteristics:

1. Political instability.

2. The central bank does not do a good job of keeping growth stable.

3. The economy is reliant on commodities.

It's fairly easy to see why the first two points can lead to a currency being described as risky. This covers a lot of emerging market currencies like the Indonesian rupiah and the Indian rupee. South Africa may no longer be strictly an emerging market currency, but the rand is also considered risky due to continuing political uncertainty and also its economic reliance on commodities including platinum and gold.

That leads me to the impact of commodities on certain currencies. Australia and Norway are both politically stable and their economies are fairly healthy. However, the Aussie dollar and the Norwegian krone are considered to be at the risky end of the FX spectrum. This is because their economies rely heavily on their commodity sectors for growth.

Norway relies on its oil industry while Australia relies heavily on its minerals and mining sector. Commodity prices tend to be volatile and they are closely linked to the economic cycle – when the economy is booming commodity prices rise, when it slows down commodity prices tend to fall. Thus, countries that have large oil, mining, or other commodity sectors tend to suffer from extremes. This causes traders to worry as it gets harder to predict future growth, which can cause the currency to be volatile.

For example, during the financial crisis in 2008, the Aussie dollar sold off against the US dollar sharply as commodity prices crashed (see Figure 1.22).

Figure 1.22: AUDUSD (2008)

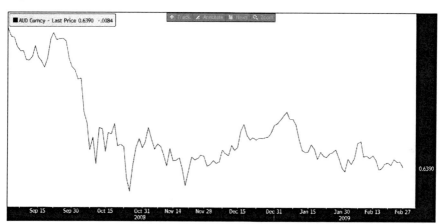

The same happened to the Norwegian krone, as you can see in Figure 1.23. Risky currencies tend to sell off particularly sharply against safe havens like the dollar during periods of market panic like the financial crisis in 2008.

Figure 1.23: NOKUSD (2008)

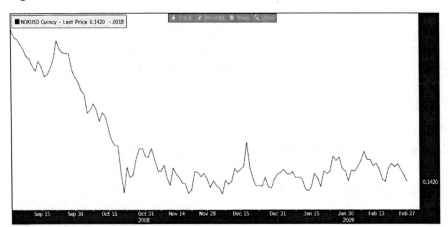

The concept of safe haven and risky currencies can make life a little easier for the FX trader as there is some certainty about what currencies will do when markets panic:

- Safe havens tend to be bought
- Risky currencies tend to be sold

FUNDAMENTAL ANALYSIS WRAP-UP

Let's summarise what I have covered in this chapter:

- *Fundamentals move markets.* You can see that currencies are sensitive to economic data and some economic signals are more important than others; in particular nonfarm payrolls in the US can set the tone for markets at the start of each month.

- *Economic data can cause an immediate bout of volatility* in markets at the moment of its release, but it can also determine longer-term trends in a currency.

- *Central bank interest rate announcements are pivotal to the value of a currency.* It's not just the change in interest rates that matters; it's the expectation of change that is the main market-moving event.

- *Central banks can intervene in financial markets*, usually to weaken their currencies, but occasionally to strengthen them.

- *Political risks can determine the movement of currencies*. The euro zone sovereign debt crisis is an example of extreme political risk that has recently impacted the forex market.

- *Safe havens and risky assets* make life a little bit easier for the forex trader.

This should give you a good overall taste for fundamental analysis, how it works and how it drives currencies. But my approach means that fundamental analysis on its own is not enough for you to become a successful trader – you need to fuse your fundamental knowledge with your technical insight.

Part B introduces the key concepts of technical analysis and how I use them to trade the FX market.

PART B
Technical Analysis

INTRODUCTION

Fundamental analysis and technical analysis are very different. Some people will stay loyal to either fundamental or technical analysis methods during their trading lives, but others dabble with both. As you already know, I am in this latter category. I will explain how I use technical analysis in my trading.

I do not intend to tell you the very basics, so you will need a grasp of these before you begin. It will be useful to have some knowledge of bar charts, candlestick charts and price patterns as I will be using these in my examples.

If you do not have this knowledge at present then there are hundreds, if not thousands, of books and websites that can give you a run-down of the basics of technical analysis. I recommend John Murphy's website Stock Charts (**stockcharts.com**) and also Barbara Rockefeller's *Technical Analysis for Dummies*, as both give great overviews.

Before we begin I'll share with you my personal (and troubled) history with technical analysis. When I first started working in a foreign exchange dealing room grasping the fundamentals and trying to figure out what nonfarm payrolls meant for the dollar was more than enough for me to chew on. However, I was aware that there was a group of traders who didn't really bother with fundamentals. They spent their days concentrating on prices and charts, charts and prices. Sometimes their trading strategies would do incredibly well. As a firm believer of learning from others, I asked them what they were doing, which turned out to be my first foray into technical analysis (TA).

I have to say, my initial look into TA didn't last long. I couldn't see the patterns that other practitioners could and to be honest I preferred fundamental analysis and the way it used real data, from real events, like central bank decisions, economic data releases, etc., to assess the market. I failed to read the TA books I was recommended and that was it for me and TA in the beginning – a short and confused relationship.

Back then I was working for BP, which traded huge amounts of foreign exchange, some with long time horizons. This type of time frame and flow is much more conducive to fundamental analysis in my opinion. It was not until I ventured into the retail forex market that I finally realised how essential technical analysis is to the retail trader.

Time Frame & Flow

conducive

A POTTED HISTORY

The modern form of technical analysis originates from Dow Theory – this isn't some complicated trading theory or algorithm, rather it is derived from the writings of Charles Dow and his op-eds at the *Wall Street Journal*, the paper he founded.

Technical analysis is derived from Dow's observations of looking at asset prices and seeing how things traded – essentially trying to find method in the madness of financial markets. He followed prices and felt that all the information you needed to know was recorded in the price of an asset. From the price you could determine if the market was bullish, bearish or neutral.

What started with Charles Dow now has hundreds of thousands, if not millions, of devoted followers across the world and if you type "technical analysis" into an internet search engine you get millions of results. Likewise, there are hundreds of thousands of videos on the internet telling you how to master technical analysis based on looking at charts and prices, and trying to define patterns, trend lines, triggers, etc. But since no two human beings see exactly the same things, technical analysis can be just as subjective as fundamental analysis.

The key thing to remember is that technical analysis is a huge field and anyone claiming to have mastered it and have the ultimate knowledge can't be telling the truth. Like prices themselves, technical analysis is always evolving, so there is no end of the line for TA – if you practice it you are in a perpetual cycle of learning.

The dinner party explanation

Have you ever planned a dinner party menu based on what you have cooked before? The answer may be *yes* if you wanted your dinner party to be a success.

Let's say that you have cooked tomato soup, roast lamb and apple pie many times, and have been pleased with the result. You have a dinner party coming up on Saturday and so you decide to do these dishes because:

1. You know how to assemble the ingredients, how long everything takes to cook, etc.

2. You have served this food before and had good results – because these dishes have been pleasing to other dinner guests in the past you think they will work a treat for your latest dinner party.

Technical analysis is a bit like this. For some traders technical analysis can be a fail-safe way to trade the markets. Essentially, it is based on using past price data and patterns to predict future prices. Let's substitute roast lamb for EURUSD to explain this in more detail.

You observe the price patterns of EURUSD over the last 12 months. You notice that this cross tends to rise or fall by 50 pips on a normal day when there are no economic data surprises or breaking news. Also it tends to respect certain levels like 1.3000 or 1.5000. These observations give you the confidence to trade EURUSD. So, just like at the dinner party, you use what you know has worked in the past to try and get the best possible future results.

— Patterns
— Trend lines
Triggers

This is illustrated in Figure 2.1, where the horizontal line indicates 1.3000. This can be a sticky level for EURUSD and you can see how the pair traded around this level for a prolonged period.

Figure 2.1: EURUSD with a resistance line at 1.3000

HOW TO USE TA

My chief aim when using technical analysis is to determine trends in the FX market. You may have heard that the trend is your friend – it is certainly mine. A trend is constant, it is unlikely to throw up surprises and if I am confident in the strength of the trend then it can help me to make profits.

Technical analysis helps me to find out all of these things, including when a trend is starting, when it is ending and how strong it is. Put together, this information should tell me whether or not I should trade with the trend.

To determine where a price will go next I need to know what the market is thinking: is it bullish or bearish on a currency, is the market changing its mind and will the trend change? Technical analysis helps me to answer these questions.

What, The Market is Thinking
  Bullish
  Bearish
- *Is Market changing its Mind*
- *Will the Trend change*

There are thousands of technical indicators that I could look at, but I prefer to limit the number of indictors that I use. Here is my personal technical analysis toolkit:

1. Candlesticks

2. Moving averages

3. Support and resistance

4. Ichimoku clouds

5. MACD (moving average convergence/divergence)

6. RSI (Relative Strength Index)

The first four are useful to determine direction; the last two are *momentum indicators* and can be useful in determining changes in trends.

I like these six indicators for two key reasons. Firstly, because I find them less subjective than other technical indicators, thus I have greater trust in the signals that they produce.

Secondly, these signals are popular and commonly used in the analysis of the forex market. Technical analysis is about knowing what the herd is thinking and where it might go next, so it's important to use indicators that are widely used in order that I know what other traders are up to.

(handwritten notes)

- what the Herd is thinking
- Where it might go Next.

- is Four → To Determine the Direction
- MACD/RSI → Momentum indicators
  useful in Determining the changes in the Trend

CHARTS

The best technical analysts that I know are very particular about their charts and how they look. To use technical analysis in your trading you need a good charting package. Check with your broker as they may offer one on their platforms, or alternatively there are also some very sophisticated charting packages that you can buy.

The first thing I do is ensure that the size of my chart is large enough to see chart patterns and price action. I put tool bars and anything else that gets in the way of the body of the chart to one side so that I get the largest possible area to look at the price action. I tend to put tool bars at the top of the chart, including time frames (so that I can toggle between them) and drawing tools, etc.

Next, choose if you are going to use bar, line or candlesticks for your chart. I tend to use candlesticks as I find they are the best way for me to *see* prices and there are some simple candlestick patterns that are extremely easy to spot. This is good for me, since I am not that adept at spotting some of the more complicated patterns.

I find that candlestick charts work best for hourly or daily charts. For shorter time periods they can be less effective. You will see that most of the charts I look at are hourly or daily time frames. Scalping and using 1, 5 and 10 minute charts is not for me as it requires a good deal of luck (which I find sometimes to be not that forthcoming when I trade).

The last thing to set up is indicators. Some, like Ichimoku clouds and moving averages sit in the body of the chart, others like the momentum indicators MACD and RSI have a chart of their own that sits directly below the main chart. These second charts can be fairly small in size so that they don't compromise your view of the price action.

Figure 2.2 is an example of how my charts look on my desktop computer, mobile phone and laptop (they would also look like this on a tablet if I had one, but I don't).

Figure 2.2: EURUSD daily: how my charts look with candlesticks, moving averages and MACD

Now it is time to move on to how I put my technical analysis toolkit to use. Rather than break this down into separate sections for each of the technical indicators, I use a series of real-life examples to show how I use the indicators in practice to try to trade with the trend.

TRADING WITH TRENDS

The whole point of my technical analysis is to try to spot trends. The most basic definition of an uptrend is when you get a series of higher highs and higher lows; the opposite is true for a downtrend. So that's what I'm looking for.

If the market likes a currency and it is rising (the *street* calls this bullish) the currency is in an uptrend (see Figure 2.3), when it doesn't like a currency and it is falling (*bearish*) the currency is in a downtrend (see Figure 2.4). Usually I want to buy strong currencies and sell weak ones – so buy into an uptrend and sell in a downtrend.

Figure 2.3: EURUSD in uptrend

Figure 2.4: EURUSD in downtrend

I will look at uptrends and downtrends in turn here.

Uptrend

Here are three methods I use to determine an uptrend:

1. Moving averages
2. Ichimoku clouds
3. Chart patterns

1. MOVING AVERAGES

Moving averages are used to smooth out price action as they show the average price over a certain time frame. Exponential moving averages and simple moving averages are the most popular and I use simple moving averages (SMAs) myself.

SMAs come in different time frames – I tend to look at 21, 55, 100 and 200 day SMAs. As I mentioned above technical analysis can be very subjective and this is definitely the case with SMAs; I originally chose to use these particular time frame SMAs because one of my old bosses did. They have worked for me so they have stuck.

In an uptrend the SMAs should be pointing upwards. If you want to trade a healthy uptrend then you should look for a nice, steady upward sloping moving average. This suggests a low volatility trend that you could trade.

But moving averages get really interesting when trends start to change. For example, if you see the short-term moving average cross above the long-term SMA then you should sit up and notice. Shorter-term moving averages are more reactionary to changes in market direction, so when the shorter-term SMA starts to move in a different direction to the longer-term SMA then it is a sign that things are changing for that currency pair.

At the start of an uptrend you should look out for the short-term SMA (say the 21-period or 55-period) crossing above the 200-period or 100-period SMA. Looking at Figure 2.5, when the 21-day SMA crossed over the 55-day SMA in August it marked the low for this pair.

Short Term MA Are More Reactionary To Changes In Market Direction

51

Figure 2.5: EURUSD daily with moving averages

2. ICHIMOKU CLOUDS

The Ichimoku cloud technique was devised by a Japanese business journalist in the 1960s. It is particularly useful when trading the yen. It is also based on the principles of moving averages, except rather than using single lines it defines areas known as clouds that determine if a currency is in an uptrend or a downtrend.

This is one of my favourite indicators because its signals are so simple to read: anything above the cloud is a technical uptrend, while anything below the cloud is a technical downtrend. Figure 2.6 shows USDJPY attempting to break above the cloud for the first time in six months (circled area). This is a significant break and could be the start of a powerful uptrend.

Figure 2.6: USDJPY – the price action is above the cloud, indicating the start of an uptrend

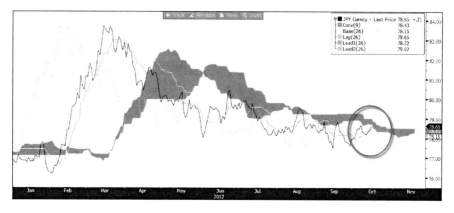

3. CHART PATTERNS

There are literally thousands of chart patterns in technical analysis. Unless you have a photographic memory then you don't stand much chance of remembering them all and spotting them in time to jump on the back of a new trend. I find it best to master a few patterns that will help me to determine if the market is in, or is about to embark on, a trend. Hence when it comes to pattern analysis I stick firstly to patterns I can recognise easily and secondly reversal and continuation patterns, as these tend to be the most accurate in my opinion.

Secondly Reversal & Continuation Patter

INVERTED HAMMER

In an uptrend, the first pattern I am looking for is called the *inverted hammer*. This is very easy to spot as the candlestick has a small lower body and a long upper wick. It shows that the bears may be starting to tire and there is some buying interest in the market to push the cross higher. It suggests that the bulls are rising out of their slumber and are about to take control of the bears. It is typically associated with the end of a downtrend and the start of an uptrend.

End of Down
start of up

The inverted hammer pattern is a signal that the downtrend may be about to end, but it does not mean that the market will turn at that moment. As you can see in Figure 2.7, it took about two weeks for the market to decisively break out of the downtrend and start on a trajectory higher after the inverted hammer pattern occurred (circled area).

Figure 2.7: EURUSD: inverted hammer pattern signalling the end of the downtrend

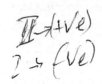

BULLISH ENGULFING CANDLE

Another key pattern that indicates a shift to an uptrend is the *bullish engulfing candle*. As shown in Figure 2.8, it is a series of two candles – the first candle is negative, and the second candle is positive and completely engulfs the first.

The second candle opened lower than the first, but it closed higher, suggesting that the battle between the bulls and the bears was decisively won by the bulls; this is another sign that a downtrend could be weakening.

1 → (+ve)
2 → (-ve)

Figure 2.8: EURUSD: bullish engulfing candlestick

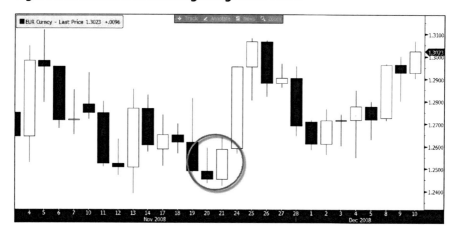

Downtrend

Most of the indicators that can be used to spot an uptrend can be used in reverse to signify a downtrend. For example, when a price falls below the Ichimoku cloud that signifies a downtrend. Likewise, there are a couple of chart patterns that also signify the end of an uptrend. One of my favourites is the tweezer top.

TWEEZER TOP

The tweezer top looks just like (yep, you have guessed it) a pair of tweezers, with two identical sized candles with small upper wicks. This suggests that a near-term top has been put in place and the price may be headed lower from there. Figure 2.9 shows an instance where a tweezer top signalled a top in the price of EURUSD.

Figure 2.9: EURUSD with tweezer top

BEARISH ENGULFING CANDLESTICK

The second pattern I watch for is the *bearish engulfing candlestick*. This is when a negative candle with a black body completely engulfs the candle immediately before it. An example of this is shown in the circled area of Figure 2.10.

Figure 2.10: EURUSD with bearish engulfing candlestick

MOVING AVERAGES

The final indicator I look at to determine a downtrend is moving averages. If the short-term SMA crosses below the long-term SMA this is a key bearish signal that suggests the price action could be headed lower.

Confirming the trend

Sometimes clouds and candlesticks are not enough and I need to find a way to confirm if there is an uptrend or downtrend. This is where the relative strength index (RSI) comes in handy.

The relative strength index is a measure of momentum in the market and is the rate of the rise or fall in an asset's price. It is the ratio of higher closes to lower closes, and is typically significant in the range 20 to 80.

The RSI is useful for two reasons. Firstly, it can help to confirm the start of an uptrend; typically this happens if the index is particularly oversold and hovering around the 20 mark. The second use for the RSI is that it can show when the market is overbought; at this point the index is hovering around the 80 mark.

Figure 2.11 shows how the RSI can be used to tell when a currency cross is overbought or oversold. On two occasions, once in September and once in December, the RSI moved into overbought territory (above 80), which was followed by a sell-off in EURUSD.

Short Term crosses Below the Long Term
→ Key Bearish Signal

Figure 2.11: EURUSD and RSI

During a trend

The biggest threat when trend-following is that the trend will end unexpectedly. A trader needs to know the difference between when a trend is merely pausing for breath (also known as the pullback), or when a trend is ending and reversing.

THE PULLBACK

Sometimes a change in direction does not signal a change in trend. One of the key things I try to remember is that the market does not go up or down in a straight line. Instead it can experience pullbacks or trade sideways for a while before trending once more.

Figure 2.12 shows EURUSD in a downtrend, but you can see periodic bouts of strength (pullbacks) in the circled areas. The market starts to move counter to the prevailing trend and then reverses and continues the trend once more.

Figure 2.12: EURUSD in a downtrend

Imagine this scenario – one day the market is trending upwards as I expected, but the next day it starts to decline. What should I do? Don't panic. This could be just a normal pullback.

So how can a pullback be identified?

I find that the best way to identify a pullback is to use channels. Figure 2.13 shows a downward channel and an upward channel. During a trend the price tends to move within the upper and lower boundaries of these channels. Price action is not perfect, and on both of these examples price action has popped outside of the channel boundaries, but only for short periods of time.

Figure 2.13: Pullbacks within channels

In a downtrend you may see prices occasionally start to rise to the upper channel, thus breaking with the prevailing price action of lower highs. Likewise, in an uptrend you may see prices start to move to the lower channel. Don't be concerned; as long as prices stay roughly within these boundaries then the trend prevails.

Pullbacks happen because different types of traders have different trading plans; some people may take profit after a couple of days, some after a couple of weeks, and some hold positions for years. Thus, although the overall bias may be an uptrend (or downtrend) there will always be people selling the currency throughout an uptrend (and buying the currency in a downtrend).

CONTINUATION PATTERNS

Sometimes prices can move sideways in the middle of a trend, which can also be the market just taking a breather before it continues in its prior trend. You can spot this by looking for continuation patterns. A couple of continuation patterns that I use are ascending and descending triangles.

ASCENDING TRIANGLES

Ascending triangles can occur during an uptrend when the price action fails to make higher highs; as we mention above a series of higher highs is one of the key determinants of an uptrend. But, the difference between a continuation pattern and the end of an uptrend is that the price will still be making higher lows. So although the price is not making any more traction on the upside, it is not falling either. Eventually this triangle gets so narrow that the price breaks out to the upside, as shown in Figure 2.14.

Figure 2.14: Ascending triangle

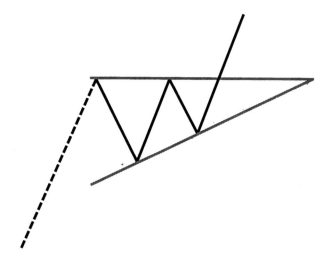

DESCENDING TRIANGLES

The descending triangle is the exact opposite of an ascending triangle. The price stops making lower lows, but neither is it making higher highs, suggesting that a breakout to the downside will eventually occur. The descending triangle pattern is shown in Figure 2.15.

Figure 2.15: Descending triangle

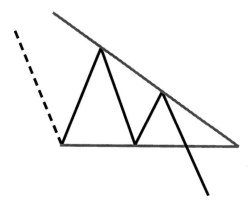

I find these triangle patterns are useful for two reasons:

1. If I have missed the first leg of a trend, triangles can present a good entry point and allow me to hop on the back of the trend at a later time. For example, in an uptrend I can wait until the market pulls back slightly. If I see lower highs, but don't see lower lows, then I may feel that the market will push this pair back to the upside, which could be an opportunity to join in. I may have missed the first leg of the journey, but there could be plenty more upside to go.

2. They can also be used as indicators to determine the end of the trend. For example, rather than breaking to the downside of the descending triangle if the price breaks to the upside then it can be a good indication that the prevailing downtrend is over and it could be a good exit point. Similarly if the price breaks to the downside of an ascending triangle it could be a signal that the uptrend is over.

When a trend ends

Once I have determined that a trend is in place and have entered a trade to take advantage of this, I am then on the lookout for signals that the trend is going to end. There tends to be two main reasons why trends cease and the market changes direction:

1. Something unexpected happens to change the outlook for the currency.

2. The trend has been played out.

Here is a checklist that I use to help me determine when a trend is about to end:

1. Do the candlestick patterns point to a change in the prevailing trend?

2. Where is the price action relative to the Ichimoku cloud – has the price fallen back inside the cloud pointing to an end of the trend?

3. What does the RSI say – is it showing the market is overbought or oversold?

Focusing just on the top point in this list, I have described some candlestick patterns below that I use to identify when a trend is coming to an end.

BEARISH HARAMI

In an uptrend you may see a bearish harami pattern, which indicates future bearish price action. The bulls have one last push higher and then the bears pile in, suggesting that a top has been put in place. See the circled area in Figure 2.16.

Figure 2.16: Bearish harami pattern

DOJI CANDLESTICK

Sometimes a change in trend can take a while to materialise, but if a trend is starting to tire there are a couple of signals that can be detected in price action. One example is the doji candlestick pattern.

A doji is when the opening and closing prices are at the same level and the upper and lower wicks are approximately the same length. This suggests indecision in the market with neither the bulls nor the bears willing to take the lead. Sometimes a doji occurs when the market is pausing for breath, at other times it is a warning signal that a trend is coming to an end.

In Figure 2.17 the doji pattern is followed by a tweezer top (circled), which is another reversal pattern and can be used to draw the conclusion that the uptrend is coming to an end.

Bullish & Bearish Harami

63

Figure 2.17: GBPUSD showing a doji followed by a tweezer top

A NOTE ON VOLUME DATA

In other markets, such as equities, you can look at volume-based indicators (the numbers of buyers and sellers) to determine the strength of a trend or if a trend is coming to an end. For example, when a trend is ending volume tends to fall off, and at the start of a new trend it tends to pick up.

There is no definitive volume indicator for the FX market because there is no central exchange. You can get volume data for the FX futures and ETC (exchange-traded currency) markets; the volume of FX futures trading is published by the Commodities Futures Trading Commission (CFTC) each week.

However, it is worth noting that this represents a small fraction of the market. Although futures traders can be fairly active participants in the FX market, the volume data needs to be approached with caution.

What happens when markets don't trend?

Considering how many times I include the word *trend* in this section you may think that markets are in a perpetual trend, but in fact this is not the case. It is said that markets only trend 30% of the time and for the rest of the time they are trading within a range (range-trading).

Throughout my career I have found that many traders label themselves – they only trade break-outs, they only follow Ichimoku, etc. I don't restrict myself in this way. If markets aren't breaking out or changing trend then you could be twiddling your thumbs for some while if you have told yourself that you don't trade at these times.

The best traders are dynamic and alter their technique according to the situation they find themselves in. This is more realistic in my view since trading styles can change with time.

An example where the break-out trader would have found the markets extremely frustrating was the first quarter of 2012, when EURUSD stayed in a range from January to May.

The upside was capped at 1.35, which was the high from November 2011. Try as it might, this pair just couldn't break above this level. However, rather than trigger another leg lower in the single currency, the cross found good support at 1.30. This pair was stuck in a range between 1.30 and 1.35 for almost four months.

Thus, EURUSD traders were forced to adapt to these range-trading conditions. Interestingly, once you have done some fairly simple legwork range trading can be surprisingly easy, as you can see in the following example.

RANGE TRADING: A REAL-LIFE EXAMPLE

STEP 1: IDENTIFY THE RANGE

Let's use the example of EURUSD for January to May 2012. As you can see in Figure 2.18, this cross tended to move higher when it touched 1.30 and sell off when it reached 1.35. A support level tends to protect a currency's downside when it sells off and resistance can thwart the upside. Thus, by looking at the chart I have identified support and resistance levels.

Figure 2.18: range-trading step 1 – establish a range is in place

More often than not you can tell by eye that a market is range trading, however sometimes momentum indicators can also give you confirmation. When markets are stuck in a range the MACD and RSI tend to flat line, showing no direction to the upside or the downside. To illustrate this, Figure 2.19 shows USDJPY in 2012 – for most of June, July August and September it was stuck in a very tight range. At the same time the RSI and MACD had both flattened out, suggesting that there was no prevailing trend in place.

Figure 2.19: USDJPY and RSI, MACD

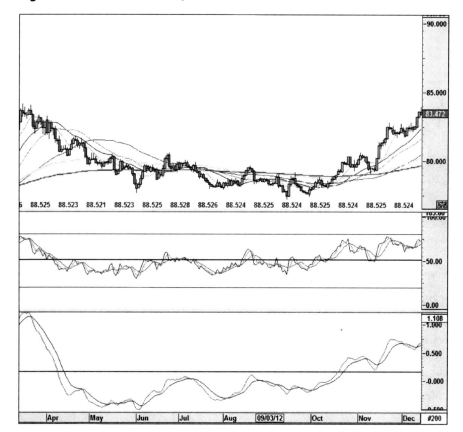

STEP 2: USE THIS INFORMATION TO PLACE A TRADE

Now I need to know what trade to place. As you can see in Figure 2.20 there are some good reversal signals in place at 1.35 ① including a triple top candlestick pattern (circled). This suggests that the market is willing to test this level but not move above it.

② Likewise, there are bullish engulfing candlestick patterns when this cross reaches 1.30 (circled), suggesting that this level attracts buying interest. I mentioned above that range trading can be simple and it is. These patterns essentially present buy and sell levels on a plate. In fact, if I wanted to hold this position for the long term then I could leave a sell order with my broker just above 1.35 for a long trade, and a buy order just below 1.30 for a short trade.

Figure 2.20: range-trading step 2 – place a trade

STEP 3: IDENTIFY WHEN A RANGE IS OVER

If the price breaks the support or resistance then the range no longer exists. One point to remember is that markets don't trade in neat support and resistance levels, so I need to leave myself a margin of error, in this example 50 to 100 pips either side should be enough. Thus, if I see EURUSD break above 1.3550 then the range would be over and the market would be entering an uptrend. Likewise, if it broke below 1.2950 a downtrend has started.

As you can see in Figure 2.21, EURUSD eventually broke to the downside in May 2012. There were signs that a downside break was on the cards. For example, EURUSD made a series of lower highs (the tell-tale sign of a downtrend) even when it was within its range. Also, after hitting 1.30 in mid-April the bulls only made a tentative effort to push the cross higher and there were multiple doji patterns forming at this time, suggesting indecision was gripping the market (see circled area).

Series of Lower Highs → The Tell Tale sign of Downtrend

Figure 2.21: range-trading step 3 – identify when the range is broken

TECHNICAL ANALYSIS WRAP-UP

There are a few things you should take away from this chapter:

1. Don't feel compelled to master all of the technical indicators out there. Choose those you are most comfortable with and stick with them. I could have used Fibonacci retracements, Bollinger bands and pivot points, but SMAs, Ichimoku clouds, support and resistance, MACD and RSI work for me. In fact some of the most successful traders that I know use little more than a couple of moving averages and MACD.

2. Technical analysis is highly subjective and is more of an art than a science.

3. The trend is your friend, but don't be put off when the markets don't trend; adopt a different approach instead, such as range-trading.

PART C

The Fusion Philosophy

INTRODUCTION

Now we come to the reason why this book was written in the first place: to show you how I look at the markets by fusing fundamental and technical analysis. If you type "using fundamental and technical analysis" into a search engine like Google, the chances are that the bulk of the results will focus on fundamental *versus* technical analysis. Commonly people compare both analytical styles and very rarely do they advocate blending them together.

Fundamental and technical analyses are often portrayed as opposite ways of looking at the market. Some people believe that the two are like oil and water – impossible to mix. However, I don't believe that is the case and I profess to be a self-taught fundamental/technical analyst of the forex market.

The problem with choosing either technical analysis or fundamental analysis is that there are weaknesses to both of these methods. Fundamental analysis can be too big a field to get a clear grasp on and depends on too many moving parts – economic data, news-flow and central bankers – for a day trader to make decisions on what currencies to buy or sell.

For its part, technical analysis can be extremely subjective. The indicators I mentioned in the technical analysis section have worked for me, but someone else may interpret the price action completely differently. Likewise, there are thousands of chart patterns that I could have filled this book with. However, I only like a select few chart patterns, as in my experience everyone sees chart patterns differently, which reduces their accuracy.

Two negatives cancel each other out, hence by combining fundamental and technical analysis you can keep the good bits about the two methods and scrap the bits that you don't like or that don't work for you.

The basic underpinning of my fusion method for FX analysis is as follows:

Fundamentals can determine the direction of a currency in the long term, while technical analysis gives you the short-term buy and sell signals.

HOW THE PHILOSOPHY WORKS

There are three things you need when you trade the FX market:

1. A trading strategy

2. Timing

3. Luck

Unfortunately I can't help you with the last point, but hopefully my philosophy will help you to nail the first two.

I was once at an industry function sitting next to an equity fund manager. He said to me he couldn't understand why anyone would want to trade currencies. "I just don't know how you can get an edge in this market," he said, exasperated after many failed attempts.

As an equity trader he was able to do in-depth equity analysis to try to root out companies that he felt were undervalued. He would look at balance sheets, scrutinise company strategy, and find out the ambitions and talents of management. If he felt, based on all of the homework he had done, that the company had potential and, crucially, if the price was right, then he bought the company's stock. For some reason he did not think this approach worked for forex.

But FX analysis *is* based on similar principles. Certain conditions have to be met before you buy or sell a currency. Just like the equity analyst you must do your homework and the concept of buy low and sell high works just as well in FX as anywhere else. However, he was right in that it is hard to get an edge in this market as the information that moves currencies is widely available and can get priced in to the market very quickly.

In my approach the homework part is the fundamentals – making sure the price is right is where technical analysis comes in. This may sound like double the work, but I will show you the most efficient way of doing this and I believe the extra effort is worth it.

As with the rest of this book, the best way to describe my philosophy is to show rather than tell how it works, so this part of the book contains a series of case studies that fuse fundamental and technical analysis.

TRADING EXAMPLES

Trading using both fundamental and technical analysis methods allows me to trade specific events, unexpected events or news headlines. These trades may have varying time horizons – some will be short term, others will be long term. Usually they are held for a minimum of one day unless stops or profit targets are triggered.

Sometimes I will have plenty of time to prepare my strategy, at other times I have to devise a strategy on the fly as events are changing quickly. Sometimes I will be right, sometimes I will be wrong.

Hopefully the case studies below give you a flavour of how I use the philosophy so that you may be able to apply some of the ideas in your own trading.

Case Study 1: USDCAD

THE BACKGROUND

In September 2012 USDCAD fell to its lowest level for more than 12 months, having declined since June of that year (see Figure 3.1).

Figure 3.1: USDCAD, daily chart

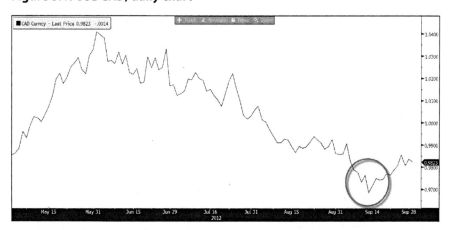

The trigger for the decline was two-fold:

1. The global macro environment had stabilised over the summer after the ECB took steps to halt the spread of the sovereign debt crisis, which helped risky currencies rally and saw declines for safe havens like the US dollar.

2. Economic data in Canada was looking resilient compared to the rest of the world (in Q2 the economy expanded at a seasonally adjusted rate of 1.9%) and there was growing expectation that the Bank of Canada (BOC) would be the first of the major central banks to tighten monetary policy in the first quarter of 2013.

However, by mid-September positive sentiment was starting to drain from financial markets. Added to this, the US central bank had embarked on a third round of quantitative easing. This made some people question just how hawkish the BOC could be.

If the BOC hiked interest rates when the Fed was still loosening monetary policy it could damage demand for Canada's exports from its biggest trading partner. Therefore, the market's view on the CAD changed from a positive view based on the potential for rate hikes and firm market sentiment to wobbly market sentiment and the prospect that the central bank could put interest rates on hold for some time.

The fundamental analyst's job at this stage is to monitor the data flow and communications from the central bank to find out how dovish the BOC really is and how likely it is they would keep interest rates on hold rather than raising them over the next few months.

THE TRADE

This is where the technical analysis comes in.

I monitor technical developments in the currency pair as well as keeping abreast of the fundamental back drop. This does not mean that I need to be stretched thin watching the charts 24/7. I try to keep an eye on the chart three times a day: one at the open, one midway through the session and one at the end of the day.

In this instance I was looking at two North American currencies, so I needed to follow their time frame (GMT -5 hours). If you are based in

Europe and you can't stay awake until the end of the North American trading day then you can check the next morning. It is also worth looking at the price chart after key data releases like PMI data, CPI, GDP and retail figures.

For this trade, by keeping up to date with the price action I noticed bullish sentiment for CAD starting to drain from the market. The first sign came on 14/15 September, when the market tried to push lower but ended up closing higher on the day. This was followed by another positive candlestick. The long lower shadow but positive body shown in Figure 3.2 (first circle), is always a warning sign for traders that the downtrend may be about to reverse.

Confirmation of this reversal came at the end of September when the daily candlestick formed a hammer pattern (second circle). This is when the body of the candle is negative but it has a long lower wick. Even though the price ended lower on the day, the bears could not push the market any lower. This suggests buying interest in the market and is a key reversal pattern.

Figure 3.2: USDCAD

Where would the market go from here? This uptrend could be as long as a piece of string, but there are a few indicators that could help me. Referring to Figure 3.3, you can see that by late October 2012 this cross was close to the top of the daily Ichimoku cloud – above this level at 0.9940 would signal the start of a technical uptrend.

Figure 3.3: USDCAD Ichimoku cloud chart

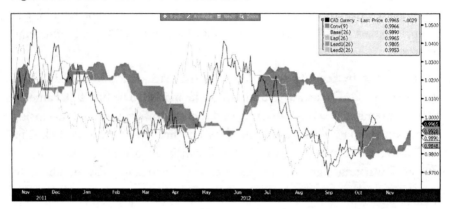

The market would always be sticky around this level. Interestingly, not only was the price approaching a key resistance level that could trigger some selling pressure, but the BOC was also holding a meeting.

The market felt that a dovish BOC was on the cards and continued to sell the CAD leading up to the meeting (USDCAD continued up). Thus, the risk was that the BOC would be less dovish than expected, thus triggering a sell-off in USDCAD (buying of CAD).

This is exactly what happened. The BOC indicated that it was concerned about indebted Canadians (hence no rate cut) and although it might not hike rates straightaway it was thinking about it. This triggered a sell off in USDCAD from 0.9980 to 0.9920.

TRADING STRATEGY

1. Buy USDCAD on seeing the reversal patterns in mid-to-late September.

2. Hold the position for the medium term as there was no fundamental reason to shift the bullish stance on this cross.

3. Combine technical and fundamental skills: on seeing the cross move to a key resistance level (the top of the daily Ichimoku cloud) I should have been on the lookout for some selling pressure. The dovish expectation for the BOC meeting would have added to my suspicions – if the BOC surprised the market and was less dovish than expected, USDCAD could experience a sharp sell-off.

4. What to do: consider taking profit at 0.9920-30 ahead of the BOC meeting. This is a major resistance zone.

Case Study 2: USDJPY

THE BACKGROUND

After the US central bank announced its third round of quantitative easing in the middle of September 2012 the market started to act strangely. Rather than weaken on the back of the Fed's pledge to buy unlimited mortgage-backed securities, the dollar started to exhibit signs of strength, particularly versus the yen. Usually USDJPY weakens with stocks and commodities, but not so this time.

Here are some of the fundamental reasons for USDJPY strength:

1. Treasury yields were starting to move higher, which USDJPY closely tracks.

2. US economic data had started to pick up, including labour market data, industrial survey reports, housing data and retail sales. If the economic data continued in this strong vein towards the end of the year then QE3's lifespan may have been short.

3. Economic data in Japan was starting to deteriorate rapidly. A territorial dispute between China and Japan had hurt Japanese exports to China as consumers avoided Japanese-made products. Exports, an important contributor to the Japanese economy, declined more than 10% in September 2012 and the prospect of a pick-up was slim. Added to this, deflation gripped the economy and business confidence had been tracking lower.

4. The weak data in Japan heightened expectations of some aggressive easing from the Bank of Japan, including large-scale asset purchases and further attempts to weaken the yen.

As a fundamental analyst with a time frame of two to three weeks I have to decide:

1. If US economic data was likely to continue to strengthen

2. How strong the prospect was of the Fed cutting QE3 short

3. Whether I believe the BOJ would embark on aggressive monetary policy accommodation going forward. This requires looking at the economic data releases and analysing central bank communications.

Essentially I am trying to find out if USDJPY has further upside during this time frame or if it is time to sell.

From a fundamental perspective, I may decide that Japan's economic fortunes looked worse than the US's and its central bank would embark on more aggressive monetary easing to weaken the yen and thus boost exports. The last thing to look at is the chart of USDJPY and the US-Japan interest rate differential as the two move closely together. This is shown in Figure 3.4.

Figure 3.4: USDJPY and the interest rate differential

This chart confirmed my fundamentally-built assertion that USDJPY may move higher. The rate spread is moving in the dollar's favour, which supports further USDJPY gains. It has already had a big upward move, so when should I enter this trade? Time to move to technical analysis.

THE TRADE

After breaking above the daily Ichimoku cloud at the start of October this pair was in a technical uptrend. The next step is to identify the strength of the uptrend and then any resistance levels of note that could thwart the bulls.

The first thing I did was take a look at the long-term momentum indicator on the daily USDJPY chart. To do this I used the Relative Strength Index. See Figure 3.5.

Figure 3.5: USDJPY, daily chart

The RSI suggests that this cross is starting to look overbought. This tells me that I might be a bit late to the party and should wait for a pullback before I enter a long position.

The next step is to identify potential support levels that could act as good entry points. The nearest level is 79.65 – a recent low. Below here the level is 78.80 – a triple top that dates back to September that should act as fairly solid support. These levels are shown in Figure 3.6 with a line and a circle respectively.

Figure 3.6: USDJPY, daily chart

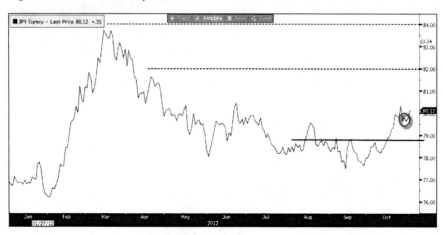

Now that I have identified entry levels, it is time to start looking for potential profit targets. Two key resistance levels can be seen on the daily chart: firstly 82.00 – the high from April, then 84.00, the high from March. These levels are also marked in Figure 3.6.

TRADING STRATEGY

1. Wait before buying USDJPY as the market looked over-extended.

2. Identify potential entry levels on the daily chart. Support levels can work well for this.

3. Plan the exit the moment the trade is considered. Are there long and short-term resistance levels that could be targeted (depending on the time horizon of the trade)?

Case Study 3: GBPUSD

THE BACKGROUND

The UK economy had a terrible first half of 2012 and was plunged into its first double dip recession for 30 years. During the third quarter of the year things started to pick up. The service and manufacturing sector PMIs surprised to the upside, the economy created jobs at its fastest pace for 20 years and inflation fell, helping to boost retail sales.

Thus, leading up to the release of the Q3 data economists were looking for a healthy rebound of 0.6% for GDP, after a 0.4% contraction in the second quarter. In fact the data was stronger than that – the actual expansion was 1% for Q3, the fastest pace of growth for five years!

However, there was a catch – some of the growth was down to one-off factors like an extra working day in Q3 relative to Q2 because of the Queen's Diamond Jubilee and there was a boost from ticket sales for the 2012 London Olympics.

Even the Office for National Statistics found it hard to quantify exactly what effect these events had on growth, but some economists deemed the actual growth rate to be more like 0.3% to 0.4%. While this is a big improvement from the second quarter it is more moderate than the 1% headline figure suggested.

This made it hard to determine the impact of this data on sterling. To complicate matters even further, the Bank of England had been expected to boost their asset purchases the following month. As a fundamental analyst I had to ask myself a couple of questions before I dived into a sterling trade:

1. Is this pace of growth sustainable? As mentioned, the answer is most likely no, due to the one-off factors. Also the more realistic 0.3% to 0.4% of underlying Q3 growth is still subject to downside risks due to the continued economic weakness in the euro zone, the UK's largest trading partner.

2. Will this data cause the BOE to halt its QE programme at its next meeting? The better tone to the economic data definitely makes it harder to justify more monetary stimulus, however the governor of the BOE at the time, Mervyn King, was still a fan of QE.

Thus, the fundamental analysis is painting a fairly mixed picture for the future price movements of sterling.

The interest rate differential between the UK and the US, which moves fairly closely with GBPUSD, though mildly sterling positive, was not giving a clear indication of where GBPUSD would go next, as shown in Figure 3.7.

Figure 3.7: UK-US 10-year bond yield spread and GBPUSD

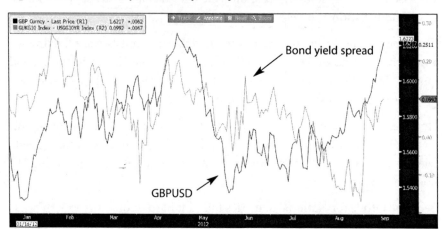

THE TRADE

There are a couple of ways to trade sterling in this environment. I could have become a buyer after a few of the data prints started to come in during August and September in anticipation of sterling appreciation, or I could have waited for the actual data release itself.

GBPUSD was extremely volatile around the time of the release of Q3 GDP, however, if I was long sterling, I would have been profitable. This is shown in Figure 3.8.

Figure 3.8: GBPUSD

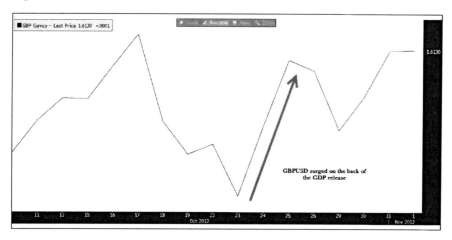

Let's say I decide to trade the actual Q3 GDP release. A few days before it would be worth taking a look at how sterling had been trading over the last month or so. I identified key levels of support and resistance as well as determining the prevailing trend. This is shown in Figure 3.9.

Figure 3.9: GBPUSD – daily chart a couple of days before the GDP release

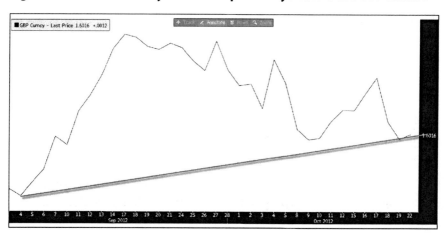

What you should notice from Figure 3.9 is:

1. GBPUSD is in an uptrend

2. There is good support at 1.5950

3. This pair has been running into some resistance recently suggesting that 1.6300 – the 12-month high – is a key resistance zone

You may also recognise the beginnings of an imperfect ascending triangle, although I think the support and resistance lines tell a good enough story that we don't need to get any more technical than this.

So what should I do?

I was expecting a big number from the GDP data release, yet sterling had been falling along with broader market sentiment in recent days, so it might be worth looking to pick up GBPUSD on dips to around 1.5950. If GBPUSD broke decisively below this support zone (shown in Figure 3.10) then going long would be a bad strategy.

So, I could look to profit on a big GDP number that would push GBPUSD back towards 1.6300.

The day after the unexpectedly positive GDP data, GBPUSD was continuing to move higher, and was above 1.6100. The next major level to watch for is 1.6200 – a support zone from late September. If the market can get above this level then it may have a chance at re-testing 1.6300. Thus, it is worth keeping an eye on this cross as there are a couple of profit-taking opportunities.

If GBPUSD does break above 1.6200, then 1.6300 is a major resistance zone and is a triple top for this pair. Unless something big happens on the fundamental front (a shift to a more hawkish stance from the BOE, for example), it would require a very big push from the bulls to break this level. I would consider taking profits at around 1.6260.

If 1.6300 is decisively broken in the coming weeks then I would look to re-enter a long trade, but keeping hold of the trade in the hope that this level will be cracked this time around is too risky for me.

Figure 3.10: GBPUSD

TRADING STRATEGY

1. Find out what the market expects from the Q3 GDP release and why. Also, look for important levels on the GBPUSD chart that could be useful before entering the trade.

2. Look to buy sterling on dips.

3. Be aware of key resistance levels. To get above major long-term resistance levels like 1.6300 then the fundamental backdrop may need to get more GBP positive. If that does not seem to be happening it might be worth taking profits approaching this level and re-entering if it makes a break higher.

Case Study 4: AUD

THE BACKGROUND

The Aussie dollar belongs to the bloc of commodity currencies that tend to be sensitive to the overall risk environment. Australia is a large producer of commodities so it is no wonder that AUD moves with:

1. The commodity price

2. The strength of its export partners who buy the commodities that Australia produces.

These factors also determine Australian monetary policy.

Figure 3.11 shows the close relationship between AUDUSD and the commodity sphere.

Figure 3.11: AUDUSD and the Thomson Reuters/Jefferies commodities index

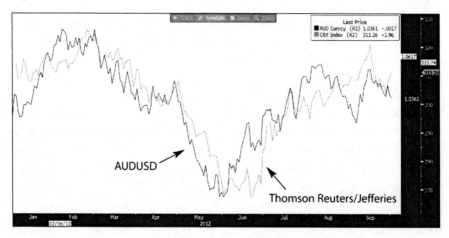

Figure 3.12 shows how AUDUSD also moves closely with interest rate differentials.

Figure 3.12: AUDUSD and the interest rate differential between Australian 10-year government bond yields and US 10-year government bond yields

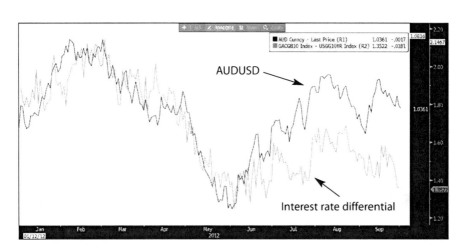

From a fundamental perspective the odds had been stacking up against the Aussie since the first few months of 2012. For example, commodity prices had been falling, China – its biggest trading partner – had seen its economic growth slow, its mining boom looked to be over and then the Reserve Bank of Australia embarked on a rate cutting cycle.

There was little to suggest the Aussie was going to rally any time soon. Instead, China had still not embarked on more monetary policy stimulus to try to boost its economy and the RBA remained in dovish mode. In this instance the fundamentals are not giving us a particularly good picture of the Aussie. It is time to check the technical picture to see if it is saying the same thing.

THE TRADE

AUDUSD is sensitive to risk, and as such can be jostled around by overall market factors alongside domestic ones. This can help the cross to remain stronger than the fundamentals would suggest. As you can see in Figure 3.13, AUDUSD was trading in a range from July to October 2012.

Figure 3.13: AUDUSD range-bound (July to October 2012)

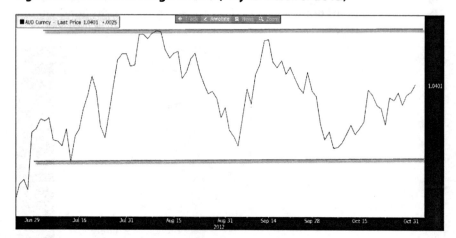

There are two things that I notice from this chart:

1. The medium-term range is 1.0180 on the downside and 1.600 on the upside. When it is in the middle of the range as it is now, I would keep it on my watch list rather than try and embark on a trade straightaway.

2. I am interested in the recent series of higher lows – that suggests to me that this cross could make another stab at 1.0600. However, I would not embark on a long until it had decisively broken above 1.0410.

LOOKING AT OTHER AUSSIE CROSSES

Sometimes the best trading opportunities are not always found when you only trade your chosen currency against the US dollar; sometimes it pays to look outside of the box. For example, while AUDUSD was stuck in a range, sterling was continuing to climb against the Aussie and remained in an uptrend.

A long GBPAUD trade offered another opportunity to trade the Aussie. This cross might have been more enticing for some traders than AUDUSD since it was still in an uptrend. A GBPAUD long trade had a strong fundamental basis as the interest rate differential between the UK and Australia had been narrowing of late, which should be GBP supportive. The RBA in Australia was embarking on a rate cutting cycle, while the Bank of England had kept rates on hold. This gave the pound the advantage over the Aussie dollar as you can see in Figure 3.14.

Figure 3.14: GBPAUD and the UK-AU interest rate differential

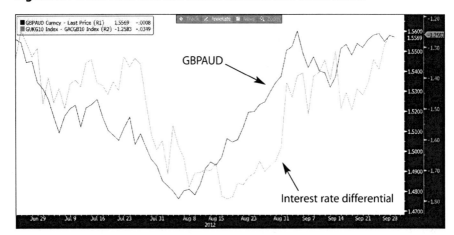

So what about the technical picture? For this I am going to look at the daily Ichimoku cloud chart (see Figure 3.15) for GBPAUD to get a sense of:

1. The prevailing trend

2. Some key levels to watch out for

Chart 3.15: GBPAUD

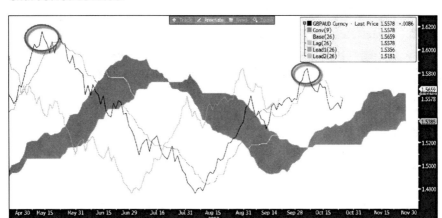

Figure 3.15 shows GBPAUD is still in a technical uptrend. After falling back from 1.5900 it managed to stay above the top of the cloud, which is now key support. There are also a couple of key resistance zones to watch including 1.5900 and also 1.6200 – the high from May 2012 (these are circled in the chart).

Recent price action has been bullish, including the last candlestick, which is a bullish engulfing pattern. This suggests that the bulls are on the side of GBP and there may be further upside for this pair.

At this stage I have two options:

1. Wait for a pullback to get in at a better level, or

2. Jump on the trend now looking for further upside and a re-test of the 1.5900 prior highs.

Usually I am an advocate of waiting for a better level – after all, only fools rush in. However, you could argue that the decline has already happened, and after holding support above the top of the daily Ichimoku cloud this is a good entry point. Either way, my first target would be 1.5900. Only if the price successfully clears this level would I hold the position to test 1.6200.

TRADING STRATEGY

1. Evaluate the fundamentals behind AUD.

2. Next look at the technical picture. If this looks better/worse than the fundamentals then I would ask myself why.

3. Sometimes you need to look beyond the focus of your initial analysis. So rather than trade AUDUSD in this case, which happened to be stuck in a range, I looked to other crosses. For example, there was an uptrend in GBPAUD that still looked constructive.

Case Study 5: Gold

This case study is about gold. It is not exactly a currency, but some people trade it a bit like a currency. Gold is often priced in dollars and so it is sensitive to price movements in the US currency. Some people also believe it is a viable alternative to fiat money (what we call today's currencies). In the past the value of money was determined by gold, but that system was ended in the 1970s.

Thus, the yellow metal has a close relationship with the FX world and many FX brokers also allow you to trade precious metals alongside FX.

THE BACKGROUND

Gold is very sensitive to changes in US monetary policy because it is traded in US dollars, so when the dollar is weak the price of gold tends to move higher as you need more dollars to buy an ounce of gold (and vice versa when the dollar is strong).

During the summer months of 2012 the US economy showed signs of slowing down and the Fed started to sound concerned about the rising unemployment rate and slowing growth in job creation. Some Fed members, including the Governor Ben Bernanke, started to drop hints that more QE may be on the cards. On 13 September the Fed announced it would embark on its most aggressive form of QE in its history and would make unlimited asset purchases.

This caused the dollar to fall sharply, and gold to soar.

THE TRADE

Gold's relationship with the dollar means it is sensitive to QE. Thus, the moment that the Fed started throwing some hints that more QE was on the cards, traders should have started to monitor the gold price. This is also where technical analysis can be used.

After peaking in February the gold price had fallen from just below $1800 per ounce to below $1550 at the end of May. Not a small decline in three months! However, it was starting to look oversold. If there wasn't a fundamental driver to keep the gold price weak then maybe it was about to change trend.

As you can see in Figure 3.16, during the summer months there were some tentative signs that gold was starting to recover at the same time as some Fed members were dropping hints about the possibility of more QE.

The first thing to notice is that the low in gold price was in May 2012. For the next two months it traded in a range, and gains were capped. A gold bug would have been interested in the fact that it was also making a series of higher lows, which suggested that a breakout to the upside was a possibility.

Figure 3.16: Gold daily chart

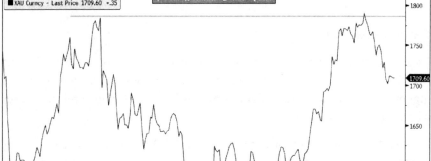

If you had monitored gold throughout the summer months, then you may have been aware that a breakout was on the cards and so decided to buy around $1580 – after another higher low in early July.

If you hadn't been that quick then you could have still entered a perfectly decent trade once gold broke out of the top of its range at $1600 in mid to late July. Even if you didn't buy at the bottom, you still managed to catch the break and you would have exposed yourself to plenty of upside. Figure 3.17 shows the breakout in early August.

Figure 3.17: Gold – daily chart: I have zoomed in on the break out that started in early August

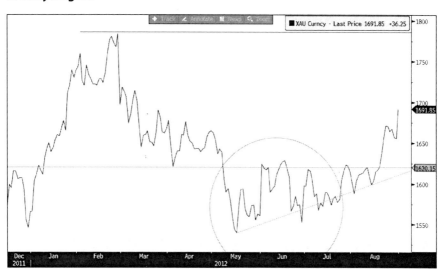

Now that you are in the trade, how long do you stay in it? There are two things I look at:

1. The fundamentals and in particular how long QE3 may have an effect on the gold price

2. Any tough resistance zones ahead that may stymie the bulls.

From a fundamental perspective, when the economic data in the US started to pick up in late September that should have been a warning sign. If QE is tied to economic performance in the US, then when the economy starts to strengthen the Fed may end QE. Thus, throughout this trade it was important to keep an eye on the US economic data releases to ensure you were aware of the latest developments.

The next thing to look for were important reistance zones. As we got to late September the gold price was approaching $1800 – the high from February. This level had stopped gold early in the year, thus it may do so again.

The potential for a premature end to QE3 from the Fed combined with a tough resistance zone at $1800 would have been good justification to exit this trade. As you can see in Figure 3.18, gold then fell to nearly $1700 per ounce over the first half of October.

Figure 3.18: Gold, daily chart – the trend comes to an end

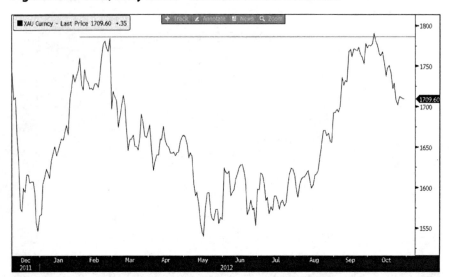

TRADING STRATEGY

1. Gold reacts to changes in US monetary policy.

2. Once the Fed started to drop hints about QE3 then I monitored the gold price.

3. Using technical analysis, a series of higher lows suggest gold could break out to the upside – this is the time to put on the trade.

4. Exiting the trade: look closely at both fundamental and technical indicators. In this case the two lined up – the US economy was picking up so QE3 may have been short lived, and gold was approaching a tough resistance zone. These were sufficient exit signals for me. After $220 of profit, I wasn't going to be greedy. It was time to book profits and exit the trade.

Case Study 6: EURUSD

EURUSD had a volatile 2012, but after reaching a high of 1.35 in February and a low of close to 1.20 in July it ended the year roughly where it had started at around 1.30. EURUSD is the most traded currency pair in the world, but the last five months of 2012 required great skill and patience.

THE BACKGROUND

The fundamentals shifted dramatically at the end of July when EURUSD was languishing close to 1.20, a level it hadn't seen since the peak of the Greek crisis in 2010. At that point the head of the ECB said that the bank would do everything in its power (as long as it was within its mandate) to protect the euro. The market saw this to mean that the ECB would stand behind the currency and protect it from speculative attacks. The euro soared.

THE TRADE

When the head of the ECB says he will protect the currency then one would expect the euro to rally. Indeed it did. Between July and October 2012 EURUSD rose nearly 10%, as illustrated in Figure 3.19.

Figure 3.19: EURUSD daily chart (June to October)

The next step was to check the technical picture. The level of 1.20 was important for this cross as it was the lowest level for two years, thus it is a technically important support zone. The fundamentals and the technicals match up for this trade, but the difficulty is jumping on the back of the uptrend in time. If you missed the boat in July, there were other opportunities, but you had to be patient.

For example, three times during August EURUSD either expereinced a pullback or a sideways move. These would have been good entry points. I have circled the potential entry points in Figure 3.20.

Figure 3.20: EURUSD daily chart

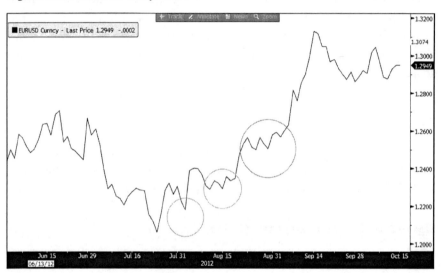

At some point you want to think about your exit. As this was such a large move, some may choose to get out after a certain profit threshold has been reached – say 200/300 pips. This is often an approach that I use.

Then if the trend is on-going I will try to get back into the trade, but I will book my profit first. The other option is to use a trailing stop loss (see the risk management section for more on this). This protects your profits through an uptrend and can be a safe way to trade in trending markets.

The other option, which is the hardest in my view, is to try to pick the top. Very few people do this with much accuracy. However, in this instance there were a couple of tell-tale signs, both fundamental and technical, that there would be selling pressure around three months after the uptrend started:

1. By September the ECB hadn't actually done anything to protect the currency bloc. Comments and pledges can only go so far. The market started to lose faith in the ECB and this weighed on the currency.

2. From a technical perspective, the failure to break above 1.32 was worrying. That was lower than the previous high in April when EURUSD reached 1.33. Thus, it suggested that the bulls may have lost the upper hand and were starting to falter.

Both of these signs scream exit to me. Not many people get out of a long trade at the very top. If you get out within 100 pips of the top that is fairly good going.

Figure 3.21 shows the culmination of the trend.

Figure 3.21: EURUSD

TRADING STRATEGY

1. If central bankers start making pledges to save a currency then take notice – it could be a spur for a change in the prevailing trend.

2. If you miss the initial move then wait for a better level to get in at. Markets pull back or move sideways even when they are trending, which can offer some good entry points.

3. Spotting the top of this trend was tough. Be vigilant. It's always important to be aware of changes in price action and the fundamental outlook in case this causes a trend to end or change direction.

Case Study 7: EURGBP

EURGBP is renowned for being particularly volatile, but it can provide some interesting trading opportunities. Back in July 2012, just before the ECB made its pledge to protect the euro, it was at a multi-year low below 0.7800. Thus, it looked ripe for a recovery or relief rally just as the ECB made its pronouncement about the euro. Figure 3.22 shows EURGBP for 2009 to 2012.

In this trade the technical reason to buy EURGBP came before the fundamental reason. That is fine – when technical and fundamental drivers meet it can mean a powerful reversal for some crosses.

Figure 3.22: EURGBP (2009 to 2012)

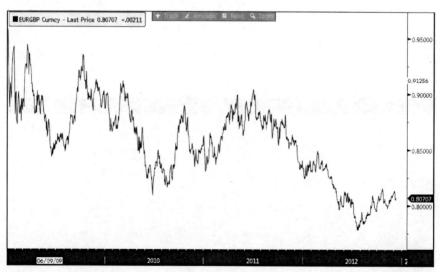

THE TRADE

The reason to go long EURGBP at this stage was driven by the technical picture first. Back in mid-2012, EURGBP had reached its lowest level since 2008. This made me wonder if the cross was oversold and due a pullback. From a fundamental perspective it was fairly easy to see why the euro was so weak against GBP:

1. The sovereign debt crisis was unresolved and threatened Spain and even Italy, the third and fourth largest economies in the currency bloc.

2. Sterling was benefitting from weakness in the euro zone. As investors were cutting their positions in the euro zone they wanted to get exposure to other parts of Europe including the UK and Switzerland. This helped to boost GBP.

After selling off sharply since early July the technical signals said this trend may be due a break, while the fundamental signs said that there could be further weakness to come.

The pledge from the ECB (see case study 6 for more detail) at the end of July shifted the fundamentals more in line with the technical signals and made this an interesting long trade in my view. Figure 3.23 shows the low in late July in more detail.

Figure 3.23: EURGBP

As you can see this trend wasn't smooth and it was a bumpy ride. At some points I was tempted to get out. However, even when the pullbacks were sharp and unexpected, as long as the cross kept making higher lows, I decided to stay in the trade. Figure 3.24 shows the development of the trend.

Figure 3.24: EURGBP making higher lows (August to September 2012)

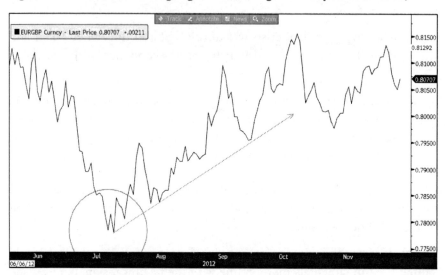

At the end of October I thought I spotted a pattern on the chart that can signal a reversal – it is called a head and shoulders pattern and is shown in Figure 3.25. This pattern – with the right and left-hand *shoulders* roughly level, and a peak in the middle for the head – can suggest a break to the downside if the cross goes through the *neckline*, which is the horizontal line on the chart.

I decided to get out at that point – just below 0.80. I felt that the technical picture was telling me that the uptrend had come to an end, added to that some market commentators had started to doubt the strength of the pledge made by the ECB.

Figure 3.25: EURGBP with head and shoulders pattern

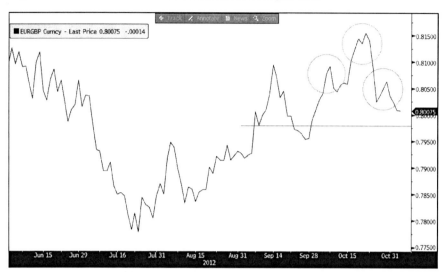

I ended up being wrong. EURGBP didn't fall through the neckline, it bounced off it. I got out too quick and ended up missing another 150 pips of profit. This is illustrated in Figure 3.26.

Figure 3.26: EURGBP

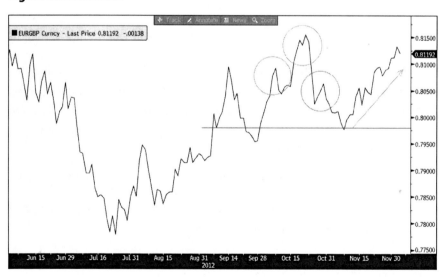

In the event this trade was still profitable, just not as profitable as it could have been.

TRADING STRATEGY

1. The fundamentals initially said one thing and the technicals said something else. Eventually the fundamental picture changed after the ECB's pledge to save the euro. This convinced me that I was right about this trade.

2. I set myself some rules: the trade was choppy, but I used a stop loss and I also said I would stay in for as long as it made a series of higher lows (the key characteristic of an uptrend).

3. I was wrong-footed by a head and shoulders pattern and got out of the trade too early. I decided not to get back in as I felt it was too choppy for me. I could have made more profit, but I misread the signals and was glad to get out and use my energy looking for another trading opportunity.

FUSION PHILOSOPHY WRAP-UP

By using fundamental analysis alone you miss out on key buy and sell signals given by the price action. By only using technical analysis you miss the broader context in which a currency is trading, which can leave you unaware of some major events that could cause volatility in the price action.

There are pros and cons of each type of analysis, but the main message of this book is to advocate fusing the two methods to get the best bits of both and improve your trading. You may have met hard-core technical analysts who sneer at fundamentals and think they are a waste of time. Likewise you may have met fundamental analysts who think that technical traders are taking the easy route out and don't want to do the hard work that fundamental analysis entails.

My theory does not ask you to sign up to one method or the other. I don't believe that is a practical way to approach your trading. To be a good trader in the FX market you can't afford to ignore fundamental or technical methods – you need to know both.

The case studies above were designed to show you how my trading strategy uses economic data, central bank decisions and communications, and breaking news, alongside support and resistance levels, Ichimoku clouds and moving averages.

This section was arranged to show that I look at the market in a particular order:

1. Find out the background and context of the market: what currencies are strong at the moment, which are weak? This is the fundamental part.

2. What does the price action look like – should I dive into the market now or wait to find a better level? What will that level be?

I find that for the majority of the time determining the context and the fundamental backdrop needs to come before the technical analysis. But for success in trading it is important to always be flexible – as shown in case study 7, sometimes the technicals come first.

In Part D I move on to look at risk management, which is the final aspect of my trading approach.

Background and the context

PART D

Risk Management

Leverage

→ Margin Requirements

INTRODUCTION

Risk management is the most important part of trading. You have probably heard this hundreds of times from brokers, blogs and other books on trading. I would go one step further and say that your risk management strategy defines you as a trader. Without it, you are nothing more than a gambler.

In trading there are losses and if you want to succeed you must accept this fact. You will probably lose on more than half of your trades, but a good risk management plan means that you can still make money even if you lose more trades than you win.

In this chapter I will not go into great depth about the concept of leverage in the FX market or margin requirements. There is a wealth of information out there on these concepts. A simple internet search can give you concise explanations. I recommend Baby Pips (**www.babypips.com**), Investopedia (**www.investopedia.com**) and *Currency Trading for Dummies* by Brian Dolan as good resources for beginners.

Likewise, you won't find any complex calculations for working out position sizes in this chapter. There is plenty written about this already and most brokers will provide you with position size calculators. Instead I will give you the risk management rules that I think make for the best trading. I will use case studies to show how risk management techniques fit into my trading approach.

TOP FIVE RISK MANAGEMENT TIPS

Here are my five steps for fail-safe risk management:

1. I use fundamental and technical analysis to determine which currencies to go long and short.

2. Once I have decided on which pair to trade I limit my maximum loss by giving the trade a cut-off point. This is also called a stop-loss and determines how much I am willing to lose on this trade if the market goes against me.

3. When I have decided how much I am willing to lose I then need to set a profit target – how much do I want to win from this trade? The combination of stop loss and profit target is known as a *risk/reward strategy*.

4. Trade size is the next thing to nail down. I need to ensure that all of my trades are appropriate for the size of my FX account. Professionals usually only risk 2% to 3% of their total capital on any one trade and this is a good rule to stick to when trading FX.

5. I try to manage my emotions and don't stray from my risk management plan.

I will now show you how I put these tips into practice with a trading example.

TRADING EXAMPLES

Case Study 1: EURUSD

BACKGROUND

It is July 2012 and EURUSD has started to look extremely oversold.

Action from the ECB looks like a credible attempt to reduce credit risk in the currency bloc's peripheral nations. Since the euro is sensitive to changes in perceived credit risk in the peripheral member states, the ECB's proactive efforts combined with oversold signals in EURUSD make me want to go long.

There is also a technical signal that makes me think maybe the downtrend is starting to fizzle out (see Figure 4.1). In the first week of July there is a bullish harami pattern – a small positive candle comes after a long down candle. This suggests that the market tried to push the euro lower, however the bullish sentiment was weak and could not be sustained. The bullish harami pattern is one of the first signs that a trend could be changing. When I see this pattern I start to think about going long, which is just what I did.

Figure 4.1: EURUSD

RISK MANAGEMENT STRATEGY

There are three stages to this:

1. Find a good entry and exit level, along with a stop loss to limit my losses

2. Decide how much I am willing to lose on this trade

3. Calculate the correct position size for my risk tolerance – basically ensuring that I don't lose more than I have planned, or more than I could afford.

So the first thing to do is find my levels. I want to enter this trade in the first week of August when EURUSD is trading at 1.2225. I now need to find a good stop loss level. The bullish harami bottom that I identified in Figure 4.1 is at 1.2060, which would allow me to put a stop at that level 165 pips away (1.2225 - 1.2060 = 0.0165).

To ensure that I can lose more trades than I win and still retain a profit I need to ensure that my profit target is at least twice as large as my stop loss. In this example I would want to aim for a 330 pip profit at 1.2555 as my first profit target. Figure 4.2 shows the chart of EURUSD with my stop loss and take profit targets marked.

Figure 4.2: EURUSD with stop loss and take profit levels

POSITION SIZE

So I know how much I want to risk and what my stop loss and take profit levels are. The next thing I need to do is decide how much of my trading capital I want to risk. After all, that is what trading is all about: deciding how much I would be willing to risk on this trade in an attempt to make a profit.

As I mention above, a good rule of thumb is to only risk 2% on any one trade. Hence, if I have a £10,000 account then I only want to risk £200 on this trade. To ensure I only risk this amount I need to place my stop loss at a level that is appropriate for my entry level.

I like to use a position-size calculator to figure out the optimal size of my trade. At this stage it is worth pointing out that FX is traded in lots; for example you buy or sell 1 lot of EURUSD. However, lots come in different sizes. A standard lot of EURUSD is the equivalent of trading $100,000, however you can also trade mini-lots that are the equivalent of $10,000. In this example I will trade mini-lots of EURUSD. These are more appropriate for my risk tolerance levels, as I only want to risk 2% of my capital base on each trade.

Now I am ready to calculate how many mini-lots I can buy to ensure that I don't breach my risk limits. Here is a quick and easy guide.

Most brokers now offer position size calculators so I don't really need to do this long-hand. However, it is worth understanding the workings behind the calculations.

The first thing is calculate how much I want to risk:

2% of my £10,000 capital base = £200

Since I am trading EURUSD contracts worth $10,000, each pip is worth $1. Remember, the pip value is quoted in dollars since USD is my counter-currency in this cross.

I am willing to risk 165 pips on this trade. Since my FX account is in pounds, it is more useful for me to find the per pip value in GBP. Let's say for argument's sake that the GBPUSD exchange rate is 1.6000, this means that each pip is worth GBP0.6.

Since I am risking 165 pips, 1 mini-lot of EURUSD would cost me GBP99 if the trade went against me:

165 x 0.6 (per pip value in GBP) = £99

That means I can trade two mini-lots of EURUSD and only risk GBP198, which is within my risk tolerance level of GBP200 (it is less than 2% of my £10,000 account).

A QUICK WORD ON MARGIN AND LEVERAGE

It is worth bringing up margin and leverage at this stage. When you trade FX you trade on leverage. That means you only need to put up a relatively small amount of capital to get a much larger exposure to the market. For example, if I trade 2 mini-lots of EURUSD I am trading the equivalent of $20,000 while only risking £200 of the cash in my account. Some brokers offer leverage in excess of 100:1, which means on a £10,000 account you can have access to £1,000,000 worth of FX contracts.

However, for the privilege a margin requirement has to be put up in the form of a minimum balance in your account. Brokers shouldn't allow you to have a negative balance in your account, and will liquidate your positions before you get into negative territory. So watch out, and always make sure you have enough margin in your account to stay in your positions.

CONCLUSION

In this example, I would buy 2 mini-lots of EURUSD with an entry level of 1.2225, a stop loss at 1.2060 and a take profit level at 1.2555 (using a 2:1 risk/reward ratio). The size and risk parameters of this trade ensure that I am only risking 2% of my capital (£200).

Case study 2: trailing stop loss

WHAT TO DO DURING THE TRADE

The middle of a trade is always a difficult time. I don't want to forget about the trade but, equally, I don't want to start fiddling with it because I'm bored. Here are a couple things I do with my time whilst in the middle of a trade:

1. Keep up to date with the economic data and the news-flow that is relevant to the trade. For example, if I am trading EURUSD I make sure I keep an eye out for the latest payroll data in the US, euro zone PMI reports, and ECB and Fed meetings. I ask myself whether the data or central bank meetings have changed the landscape for the currency and whether it will impact the trade?

2. I keep an eye on the charts. If you are a medium-term trader with a trade horizon of a few weeks then it is worth checking the charts at least once a day. If your time horizon is shorter then consider checking the charts more frequently.

WHAT I DO IF THE TRADE IS GOING IN MY FAVOUR

Let's say I bought 1 mini-lot of EURUSD and the trade is going in my direction – I stand to make a profit. What should I do now? This is tricky.

Why come out of the trade if I think that the trend is going to continue? However, I have a plan and I should stick to it, right? Well, yes, but all good plans need a little tweaking sometimes. That is where the trailing stop loss comes in.

Using the example in Case Study 1, I entered a long EURUSD trade at 1.2225, my stop loss is 165 pips away at 1.2060 and I have a 2:1 risk/reward ratio, which means that my profit target is 1.2555.

Let's say the market moves up by 90 pips to 1.2315. The market is going in my favour, but I have now exposed myself to 255 pips of loss as my stop loss remains at 1.2060. If the market moves against me now, I could potentially get stopped out and lose the initial gains I had made.

To avoid this situation, after a sizable move in my favour I move my stop loss. Most brokers will allow you to move your orders around while you are in a trade; get your sales representative to talk you through it if you are uncertain of how to do it.

If I move the stop up to 1.2265 (giving myself a 50 pip stop on the price at which EURUSD is currently trading) then I would have made a guaranteed profit from the trade, since my stop loss is now 40 pips above my original entry point at 1.2225.

Although you can rest easier when you use a stop loss, the opportunity to trail stop losses and lock in profits is a good reason why you shouldn't ignore your trade. I check on a trade at least once or twice a day (preferably three times if possible) to see if it is going in my favour. I actively manage my trades and move my stop loss if the risk/reward ratio starts to go out of whack.

Some brokers offer an automated trailing stop loss. You specify the amount of pips and the system moves your stop loss to ensure it is always that far away from the current price. This removes a time-consuming manual process and ensures that you don't forget to adjust your stop loss and protect your profits.

WHAT I DO IF THE TRADE ISN'T GOING IN MY FAVOUR

In Case Study 1 I added a stop loss level to my order ticket. So if the market goes against me then after a certain level has been reached I will be stopped out.

The stop loss meant that I was willing to risk £200. Losing is part of trading. The problem arises when the trend appears to change midway through the trade and I want to know what to do: stay in the trade until I get stopped out, or cut my losses now?

If there has been a large shift in the fundamentals underpinning the trade – say a natural or geopolitical disaster, a surprise shift in stance from the central bank or a raft of weak economic data – then I may decide it is better to cut my losses and get out before the stop loss level is reached.

But this does not happen often. In general I would not tinker with my trade. I made it for a reason and chose the stop loss and take-profit levels for a reason. If a trade goes against you it is not always because there has been a shift in the fundamental backdrop and the trend is changing, it may be because the market does not always go up, or down, in a straight line. Thus, I wouldn't want to close the trade too early, especially if the market is experiencing a pullback before continuing its prior trend.

Case study 3: managing emotions

In my experience how well you manage your emotions depends on the person. There is no strict formula you can apply; some people are just better at it than others.

I have worked with some professional traders who were paid a lot of money by big corporations to trade FX and if a trade went against them they would roar or shout (generally at junior members of staff) or fall into a deep depression. Likewise if a trade went in their favour they would be beaming, almost doing a lap of honour round the trading floor like an Olympic gold medallist. Both are the reactions of people who cannot manage their emotions.

This does not mean that you need a poker face when you are trading, just that you should try to keep waves of feeling at bay. The markets are capricious beasts: they like you one moment and they hate you the next. And just like the Gods on Mount Olympus they will punish hubris.

The best traders I know spend their energy doing their homework – fundamental and technical research – to get the best possible stop loss, entry and take profit levels. The best lesson I ever learnt at journalism school was that the facts are your friend. This works in most areas of life, but especially in trading.

Some experts will tell you to write a diary. In my experience writing a diary does not automatically help you to manage your emotions in a trade, but it is simple to do and can be of use. Before you put the trade on ask yourself why you are doing it and write this down. This does not need to be a long treatise. Using the EURUSD example at the start of this section you could write:

> "ECB President promises to stand behind the euro during the sovereign debt crisis, which has helped to reduce credit risk and should benefit the currency. There have also been some strong trend reversal patterns at 1.2060, which is now a psychologically important level, and suggests to me we have put in a low."

Next jot down the dynamics of your trade:

> "I am entering the trade at 1.2225, I want a 2:1 risk reward ratio and I am happy to run this trade over a number of days as I believe it could last a while. Hence, I will put my stop loss 165 pips away at the 1.2060 low and target a 330 pip profit at 1.2555."

There is no need to give an hour-by-hour status update on the trade. Instead update only any changes you make like trailing stop losses, partial profit taking, etc.

Now let's say that I eventually close out of the trade at 1.2700. However, when EURUSD breaks above 1.2810 and when it gets to 1.2950 I believe it could get as high as 1.3500. I jump in but within a few days the trend has reversed and EURUSD is falling and I am at risk of losing money. See Figure 4.3.

Figure 4.3: EURUSD (January to October 2012)

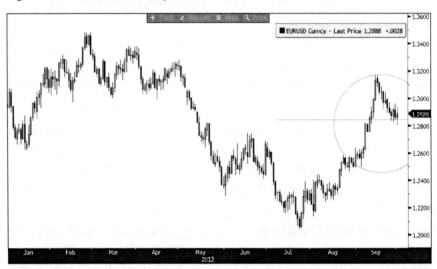

This is where a trading diary can act as a post mortem of the trade and help you to learn from your mistakes. There was no fundamental or technical reason for entering the second EURUSD trade – instead I went long because I made money on this trade before. This is a common mistake, but a deadly one. Remember: the facts are your friends. Doing well in the trade previously and having a *feeling* that it will continue to do well are not good enough reasons to enter a similar trade in the same market now.

RISK MANAGEMENT WRAP-UP

1. I always make sure there are both fundamental and technical reasons to go into a trade.

2. I use stop losses before the trade and trailing stop losses once I am in a trade.

3. I monitor the charts during a trade.

4. I manage my emotions. If you are an emotional person then remember that the facts are your friend and facts are what you need to be a good trader.

Conclusion

So you have made it to the end of the book; either you read it cover to cover or you did what I do and start with the last few pages first! This book is not designed to make you the best trader in the world, rather it is designed to show you how I do things – to help you to look at the market from a different slant – and learn how to take the best bits from technical and fundamental analysis.

In an ever-evolving forex world, the day trader can feel pushed out by high-frequency trading and algorithms. However, doing the simple things right – such as using the fundamental indicators and chart pattern techniques that I show – can still result in trading success.

Rather than finish the book with another anecdote of my history working in financial markets, I thought I would try to leave you with something useful – my top ten tips for trading. They are not all original, some of them I have collected while reading various trading books and blogs, others I have been told or wish I had been told. I hope that you find them useful.

MY TOP TEN TIPS FOR TRADING

1. **Learn, learn and learn**. Whether you are a novice or a seasoned pro, never stop learning. It's important to keep abreast of new technology that could alter the way you trade and hopefully make it easier. You also need to be aware of current trends and new economies that are growing in importance. Technical analysis is all about knowing what the *street* is thinking and to find that out you can read blogs, the financial press, look at charts, learn patterns and join trading communities. There are a lot of free resources out there and it is worth making use of them.

2. **Practice**. It can be easy to get bogged down in the theoretical detail, but once you have your strategy pinned down, put on a trade. At first it can be petrifying especially if you see your money slip away. However, you will learn how to deal with those emotions in time. Once you have a bit of practice behind you of forming a logical, well-reasoned trade idea, creating a set-up and implementing a strong risk management process, then getting a trade right can give you an immense feeling of satisfaction.

3. **Start small**. Don't ever bet the ranch, but definitely not at the start. If you are new to trading you need time to adjust to how markets and your trading platform work. You may make mistakes so don't let them erode too much of your capital base. Even a seasoned pro using a new trading strategy for the first time would go back to smaller position sizes until they get the hang of it. Start small and then build your sizes up as your capital base increases.

4. Always remember this process and etch it on to your brain: **entry level, stop-loss, take-profit and risk/reward**. This is a simple but vital risk management process that can save you a lot of headaches down the road.

5. **Don't compromise on your stop-loss or risk/reward ratio** and don't tinker with them in the middle of a trade (if using a trailing stop loss define your risk tolerance before you enter the trade).

6. **If you lose, remember that it shouldn't matter if you have a good risk management strategy.**

7. **If you don't have time to put together a proper trade set-up and implement a well-researched risk management technique then don't trade.** Come back and trade when you do have the time.

8. Remember that **fundamental analysis can give you a good idea for a trade and it can even help with timing your trade if you are using an economic data release, but you can't rely on this alone.** Technical analysis gives you entry and exit levels and stop loss levels, which are vital for your trade to perform well. This can make trading less stressful and hopefully more profitable.

9. **Cut through the jargon.** There are hundreds of technical and fundamental indicators that you could follow, but sometimes it's hard to see the wood for the trees. Slow down, choose indicators that you like and that make sense to you. If you are using technical analysis, make sure that you can always see the price action on your chart. Some of the best traders choose a couple of moving averages and a MACD and have great success. The key is to choose what you are comfortable with and stick with it.

10. **Don't let trading take over your life.** You can do it every day and love it, but trading is a very solitary activity, and you live and die by your decisions. Take time out. Life is short so enjoy spending time with friends and family away from the markets. I always find this clears my head and I get back to my desk brimming full of ideas.

I hope that you have found some of these tips useful and that they can serve you as well as they have served me.

Thank you for reading and good luck trading.

Kathleen

APPENDIX

SUGGESTED READING LIST

These are some of the resources that I look at daily. I find them useful and you may too:

- *Financial Times* (**www.ft.com**)

- *Wall Street Journal* (**www.wsj.com**)

- *The Economist* (**www.economist.com**)

- FT Alphaville (**ftalphaville.ft.com**)

- The Big Picture (**www.thebigpictureblog.com**)

- Zero Hedge (**www.zerohedge.com/blog**)

- Baby Pips (**www.babypips.com**)

- Stock Twits (**stocktwits.com**)

BIBLIOGRAPHY

Throughout my career I have read a huge amount of literature on forex (partly to make up for the lack of economics or finance degree) but these works have been particularly helpful to me during the writing of this book:

Peter L. Bernstein, *Against the Gods: The Remarkable Story of Risk* (John Wiley & Sons, 1998)

Jesse Livermore, *How to Trade in Stocks: The Classic Formula for Understanding Timing, Money Management and Emotional Control* (McGraw Hill, 2001)

John J. Murphy, *Intermarket Technical Analysis: Trading Strategies for the Global Stock, Bond, Commodity and Currency Markets* (John Wiley & Sons, 1991)

Barbara Rockefeller, *Technical Analysis for Dummies* (John Wiley & Sons, 2004)

Peter Temple, *CFDs Made Simple: A Straightforward Guide to Contracts for Difference* (Harriman House, 2009)

Index

Bold denotes a chart example